Fantasio and Other Plays

ALFRED DE MUSSET

Fantasio
and Other Plays

TRANSLATED BY MICHAEL FEINGOLD,
RICHARD HOWARD, NAGLE JACKSON
AND PAUL SCHMIDT

INTRODUCTION
BY AMLIN GRAY

TCG TRANSLATIONS

1993

Fantasio and Other Plays is published by Theatre Communications Group, Inc., 355 Lexington Ave., New York, NY 10017.

Musset, Alfred de, 1810-1857.
[Plays. Selections. English]
Fantasio and other plays / translated by Richard Howard . . . [et al.] ;
introduction by Amlin Gray.—1st ed.
(TCG Translations 4)
ISBN 1-55936-066-6 (cloth)—ISBN 1-55936-067-4 (paper)
1. Musset, Alfred de, 1810-1857—Translations into English.
I. Title. II. Series.

PQ2369.A236 1993   92-44012
  842'.7—dc20   CIP

Cover design and watercolor copyright © 1993 by Barry Moser
Design by The Sarabande Press
Composition by The Typeworks
Color separations provided by EMR Systems Communication
First Edition, April 1993

CONTENTS

Introduction

"Nothing is sadder than to arrive *mal à propos*"—inopportunely. So says the Baron in *You Can't Think of Everything*. Alfred de Musset, the author of the greatest French plays of his century, the creator of prose and verse styles that achieved a miraculous combination of spontaneity and finish, arrived in the world *mal à propos*.

He was born well, to be sure. The de Musset family had ancient ties to a multitude of notables, among them Joan of Arc and the sixteenth-century poet Pierre de Ronsard. The location of his birth, too, was propitious for a future poet: Paris. But the year was 1810.

In his autobiographical novel *The Confession of a Child of the Century* (1835), Musset writes that he was part of an unfortunate generation. "During the Napoleonic Wars, while their husbands and brothers were in Germany, the anxious mothers brought into the world a straining, pale, nervous brood. These thousands of children were conceived between battles. From time to time their bloodstained fathers would appear, lift them to their gold-laced chests, then lower them back to the ground and get back on their horses." Then Napoleon fell and the kings of Europe forced France to reestablish its monarchy. Liberty, Equality, Fraternity were now nothing but words in the mouths of the older generation. Writes Musset: "All the evils of the present come from this: that which was is no more; that which will be is not yet. Do not seek elsewhere the cause of our malady." Others diagnosed it differently, but the *maladie du siècle* was everywhere recognized. So were its symptoms: aimlessness, disorientation, ennui.

Musset did well in school and, at seventeen, he faced the standard choice of young men of his class: law or medicine. He chose medicine, but was completely and conclusively put off by his first dissection. He had already begun the love affairs he would pursue throughout his life, as well as commerce with the (by his account) thirty thousand licensed prostitutes of Paris. He was also writing poetry, and a friend got him an entree to the *cénacle* led by Victor Hugo. The *cénacles*—literary salons grandly if not blasphemously named for the room where the Last Supper took place—were centers of French cultural life.

Victor Hugo was himself quite grand. (Jean Cocteau was to say that Victor Hugo was a madman who thought he was Victor Hugo.) The French Romantic movement is commonly dated as beginning with the triumph of his play *Hernani* (1830) and ending with the failure of his play *Les Burgraves* (1843). Joining the *cénacle* not long before this thirteen-year ascendancy began, Musset was not truly part of the struggle, nor did his style develop with, and thereby come to harmonize with, the styles of the association's many gifted poets and playwrights. The movement's mission was to free literature from the conventions that had stifled it almost to death. These placed a premium on classical (Greek and Roman) subject matter; elaborate, rigid rhyme schemes; and, for plays, the strict separation of tragedy and comedy and a slavish adherence to the unities mistakenly thought to have been mandated by Aristotle. All these standards were policed by the Académie Française.

In 1829 Musset published *Contes d'Espagne et d'Italie*, a collection of poems that both excited and offended his fellow *cénaclistes*. Musset had chosen subjects dear to the Romantics—the Mediterranean (in which Shelley had recently drowned), exotic courtship, tragic vengeance, the gondolas of Venice, the moon. Often he had treated them with the expected wooziness, "becoming" everything he saw, in the fashion of the new conventions the *cénacle* had set down. But sometimes he went his own way. The big sensation of the volume was *"Ballade à la lune."*

> *Sur le clocher jauni,*
> *La lune,*
> *Comme un point sur un i.*

"Above the yellow steeple, the moon, like the dot on an i." Classicists and Romantics alike were horrified. This was not the way you talked about the moon. Nor did you ask the sacred orb if it was the one-eyed sky staring down looking for scandal, or just a big ball, or an armless spider.

Musset worked briefly at an administrative job in military procurement, but by 1830 (age twenty) he was earning his living with his pen. Prose narrative was the most lucrative medium for writers and Musset wrote *récits* throughout his life, though he found the form laborious. When, at night, he opened his windows, lit dozens of candles and invited his muse, she preferred to bring him poetry or plays.

His first work for the stage was a dramatization of an episode from Sir Walter Scott's novel *Redgauntlet*. This was accepted by the Théâtre des Nouveautés but never performed. His next play was *The Venetian Night* (*La Nuit Vénitienne*). This was played, catastrophically.

Opening night was the first of December, 1830. *Hernani* had imposed itself almost a year before and the Romanticists were riding high, but a reaction had set in. The Classicists came out in force to damn the effort of a young man whom they lumped with the movement. In the second scene, the heroine, dressed in white satin, leaned against a green trellis and looked down onto the canal with its drifting gondolas. Unhappily, the set was newly painted. When she came away, her gown displayed neat green crosshatching. The pandemonium, already high-flying, went out of control and the curtain was lowered. The second night went just as badly and the play was taken off. Musset vowed never to write for performance again.

Once more, Musset had arrived in the right place at the wrong time. *The Venetian Night* is no lost masterpiece, but it's a work of some originality. Laurette, the heroine, has been forbidden to marry the young gentleman-of-leisure Razetta. Her guardian has arranged a wedding with the Prince of Eisenach, whom she is about to meet for the first time as he arrives to take her away. Razetta threatens that unless she kills her fiancé by eleven P.M. she will have Razetta's death on her conscience. He leaves a stiletto under the foot of her harpsichord for her convenience.

The play doesn't build up much suspense. It is apparent from the outset that Laurette isn't going to stab anybody. Even Razetta seems to suggest that if she merely comes down to his gondola and floats away with him that will be perfectly adequate. She does neither, and here lies the originality of this embryo work. Contrary to both Classical and Romantic usage, Laurette goes along with the dictated marriage.

This departure from the behavior expected of a person in a play was the first instance of a pre-Shavian mechanism that Musset would use again and again. Shaw's practice was to put real people (albeit people who, like Musset's, had an unnatural flair for verbalizing their positions) in stock situations from books. Then he would let them behave as they'd behave in real life. Laurette *would* marry the Prince of Eisenach rather than a ne'er-do-well who slips her stilettos, especially since the Prince turns out to be not the expected ogre but a philosopher both forthright and fanciful. Razetta, too, acts at last like a real person. For the space of a soliloquy, he considers making good on his suicide threat. Then he climbs back into his gondola and rejoins Venice's perpetual revels.

Since Musset had vowed henceforth to write plays only for an imaginary theatre, his next two dramas were published in a volume titled *Armchair Theatre* (*Un spectacle dans un fauteuil*, 1832). One, called *The Cup and the Lip* (*La Coupe et les Lèvres*), out-Hugoed Hugo in bombast and *nouveau*-Gothic sensationalism. The other—*What Do Young Ladies Dream of?* (*A quoi rêvent les jeunes filles*)—is Musset's best-known work in America, although at two removes. The plot involves a father's attempt to make his daughter fall in love with the man of his choice by arranging an "assault" from which the young suitor can rescue her. In 1894, Edmond Rostand used this premise in *Les Romanesques*. In 1960, Tom Jones and Harvey Schmidt, crediting Rostand but not Musset, created *The Fantasticks*.

It's not hard to understand why Musset felt that, as he put it in a poem, "I came too late into a world too old." His generation, raised on values that went immediately bankrupt, was floundering. The audience for his work was highly polarized and he was at neither pole—he was on a spectrum of his own.

In 1833, his love life was to inflict on him perhaps the most painful mistiming of all. He fell in love with the former Aurore Dupin—a memoirist-novelist known by this time by her pen name, George Sand. Brilliant, sensitive, serious, original, devoted, Sand might have been, save for one accident, the perfect mate for Musset. The accident was that she'd been born six years before him. She was twenty-nine and he was, for all his whoring, a young twenty-three. She'd been married, she'd had affairs with other famous writers, she had two children. He wanted to grow side by side with Sand, but she'd grown well ahead of him. They spent their last months of cohabitation in Venice. Her working method—she was voluminously productive, an "ink-pisser" said her detractors—was to schedule long regular hours at her desk and to keep to them. His way was to wander the streets and when inspiration struck to sit down on a bench and let fly. He sought stimulation through drinking—a favorite tipple was absinthe, later outlawed as a hallucinogen—and through gambling and the company of women. His and Sand's differing habits, and other incompatibilities that violated the high standards both held for the relationship, led to furious fights. In February of 1834, Musset fell dangerously ill with malaria. Sand nursed him, finally coming to feel so much like his mother, and so little like his lover, that she embarked on an involvement with his doctor. By April the convalescent, departing for Paris, made a gesture in keeping with the selflessness he demanded of himself toward his soulmate. He had perceived the attraction between Sand and Pagello (the doctor). As he left, he put their hands together.

After Sand's return to Paris, the romance resumed and shattered several times. In March of 1835, Sand broke it off for good.

For Musset literature was never, as for Wordsworth, "emotion recollected in tranquility." He had to work while in the throes of experience. 1834, while the affair with Sand was raging, was his miracle year as a writer. In January he published *Fantasio*. In July he published *Don't Trifle with Love* (*On ne badine pas avec l'amour*). In August he published *Lorenzaccio*. All three were entangled with his feelings for Sand. The two latter, in fact, were partly taken from her words. The months with Sand, in their intensity, were the high point of Musset's life, and it accords with Musset's idea of the creative impulse that they should have given birth to his finest work.

Musset found success in failure. In this he was a true Romantic—too true a Romantic to have been truly of the movement, or of any movement. The shortfall of Musset's relationships with Sand and other women confirmed the loftiness of his ideals. And he wrote better plays than any that could have been fashioned to the standards of his time.

Musset's paradoxical success, however, was over by age thirty. He had always said it would be. As he writes in numerous places—even people in the plays cite the number—age thirty is the end of everything. After thirty, one can look ahead only to "the winter of life." His characters this age or older are, with very few exceptions, mechanical figures. Musset calls them *fantoches*—marionettes. The puppets have surrendered to the world. They let it pull their strings. At twenty-eight, Musset himself made a *fantochesque* accommodation he would never have made earlier. He appealed to the Duke of Orléans, a former schoolmate, for support of his application for a post as librarian at the Ministry of the Interior. A poem on the birth of the Count of Paris probably clinched the position for him. Fifteen years later, after this appointment had lapsed, he wrote a verse play whose ancient-Roman subject was suggested by the Minister of Education, and thereby won that Ministry's librarianship. In 1848, he campaigned for election to the Académie Française. Refused, he tried twice more and finally, in 1852, he won acceptance to a body whose conservatism he had previously scorned.

Musset's thirtysomething and fortysomething plays usually had happy endings, as the plays of his youth seldom had. This difference seems to reflect less a change of outlook than an exhausted surrender to formula. Only in short works—though very notably in some of them—did the gaiety, the stingingly fresh prose, and the free-flowing invention of his best years sometimes reappear. Among these are the delightful *You Can't Think of Everything* (*Il ne faut penser à tout*) and the perfect *A Door Should Be Either Open or Shut* (*Il faut qu'une porte soit ouverte ou fermée*). (Even the perfection of the latter could be seen as a mark of decline. The young Musset would never have stooped to writing anything *perfect*.)

In 1847, Musset's estrangement from the stage ended with the production of the brief *Un caprice* at the Comédie-Française. It did very well, and other short works began to be played. Musset adapted *Les Caprices de Marianne*, his best "armchair" play not published in this volume, in accordance with the aesthetic, moral and logistical standards then prevailing in the theatre. The result hamstrung the play, but the production was successful.

Three bouts of pneumonia over years exacerbated Musset's longtime heart condition. Finally what to him had been, by self-fulfilling prophecy, nearly half a life of half-life, petered out. He died in 1857.

■

Musset wrote some twenty-five plays. Of his four now-acknowledged full-length masterpieces, only *Marianne* was produced in Musset's lifetime, and that in his crippling revision. Most people would allow that the greatest playwrights have worked in the producing theatre, steeped in the communion of actor and audience. How did Musset, in the absence of any such contact, come by his feeling for the theatre?

By every account, he was a spellbinding reciter of his own and others' poetry, as well as a born mimic. If Arthur Miller is correct in saying that everyone else in the theatre would really like to be an actor, Musset appears to have had the right instincts.

He was also an inveterate theatregoer. (In one of his most famous poems, he describes having gone by himself to the theatre, where he didn't feel alone because the playwright—Molière!—was having a failure.) Despite his own lack of professional involvement, he wrote penetratingly about the mechanics of the art, from the director's use of stage space to how Mlle. Pressy made her effect on a certain exit in *Le barbier de Séville*. Writes the director Jacques Coupeau: "Musset saw what goes on onstage, an uncommon gift."

He did not, like many lyric poets, possess a unitary vision. He was a divided man. At age nineteen he told his brother: "I sense in myself two men, one who acts and one who watches. If the first commits some folly, the other profits by it. I play, but I am not a player." Sand saw him as divided between a devil and an angel. Talking of *Marianne*, she noted that both male protagonists were Musset: the fluent and detached Octave and the tongue-tied and embroiled Coelio. Musset had the gift, essential to a playwright, of what Keats calls "negative capability," the power fully to invest oneself in opposing viewpoints. Marianne is divided *within* herself, as are Fantasio and Lorenzaccio. Here is an even deeper expression of the internal split that equipped Musset to write for the theatre.

A play deals in the motion of time. Lessing distinguishes between painting and epic or dramatic writing by saying that the former is simultaneous—all parts of a picture are seen at once—while the latter is consecutive. Musset's description of the unfortunate children who grew up during the Napoleonic

Wars, quoted above, shows his penchant for consecutive writing: the visiting father lifts the child, puts him back down and climbs on his horse. Elsewhere, when describing a painting, Musset can't leave it static. He gives an account of the house, the well, the woman, all present simultaneously, but then his discipline breaks. He has the horsemen ride straight off the canvas.

Playwriting is the idiom of the noun and the verb. It does not describe and qualify, it shows. "Romanticism," Musset wrote, "is the abuse of adjectives." Once, for his amusement and that of their friend Sainte-Beuve, he went through Sand's novel *Indiana* crossing out all the adjectives. It was the act of a born dramatist. (Though one wonders what Sand would have thought of the exercise.)

The nineteenth-century critic Francisque Sarcey, no fan of Musset, had to admit his ingrained talent as a writer for the stage. "Take even his most vulnerable works. They are written by a man whom the fairy of the theatre touched at birth. I don't much like *Fantasio*, with its fine-drawn, contorted *esprit*. But look at the first scene where he is chatting with his friends. How well it is constructed! How every word is *en situation*! How, from one end to the other of this conversation, one is carried along by a broad scenic sweep!"

On the French stage, Musset is a proven classic. His best plays, discounting *Marianne* and *A Door Should Be Either Open or Shut*, are in this volume, in freshly coined English. One can only commend them to a large armchair audience and, still more, to producers and directors.

■

Fantasio was written in Venice in 1834. It was not produced until thirty-three years later (nine years after the author's death). Part of its inspiration was a political marriage like the one proposed in the play, the joining of "Citizen-King" Louis-Philippe's daughter to the King of Belgium. Fantasio, the brightly melancholy jester who is diverted by his own boredom, whose apparent airy negligence conceals deep thought and feeling, was immediately recognized by readers as an authorial self-portrait. Legend has it that a production was discussed in Musset's later years and that he rejected an actor for Fantasio saying, "You don't look enough like me." Of the play's posthumous premiere, a lifelong friend of Musset writes: "I confess that when I saw Delaunay come onstage, with his long light hair . . . it was as if I saw again, living, the author himself. . . . The memory of the youthful days we spent together, the nightmoths, so to speak, of our early time, came crowding upon me, flitting around the colored lanterns of Musset's fantastic Munich." Sarcey writes: "As to the character of Fantasio, Alfred de Musset released himself into his play. And it is just this for which one loves this lamented poet. In his work—poetry, drama, *récit*—it was himself, his heart, his life that he gave, with a kind of wild fever."

The 1866 Comédie-Française premiere was presented in a version by Paul de Musset. The adaptor said his brother had given him instructions for changes during his last illness. The rearrangement of scenes, the insertion of "clarifying" transitions, and the strong suggestion that a romance between Fantasio and Elsbeth would follow the final curtain did not keep it from failure. (The young Musset had led his "armchair" audience to expect a final liaison of hero and heroine, which then he expressly ruled out. Compare Shaw's ending to *Pygmalion. My Fair Lady's* reversion to the formulaic ending made that musical a hit, but Paul's revised *Fantasio* had no such luck.)

Constant Coquelin, who would create the role of Rostand's Cyrano thirty years later, played the Prince of Mantua—one of Musset's most vivid *fantoches*, an apoplectic tyrant whose two-dimensionality is at once comic and frightening.

The first production of the original text was at the Théâtre des Arts, 1911. This also failed, but critic Alfred de Tarde wrote: "People generally see in Musset only the bubbling wit, banter and youthfulness floating on the surface of his theatre; they fail to recognize the robust genius, the understanding of the heart . . . the solid and enduring structure."

In 1925, the Comédie-Française presented Musset's un-modified text and had an enormous success. Pierre Fresnay played Fantasio. The play has remained in the Comédie-Française repertoire ever since.

Richard Howard's version was commissioned by Garland Wright for the Guthrie Theater in Minneapolis. Howard states that the play's derivations from earlier writers like Beaumarchais and Mérimée "are of less significance to us now than the play's outright attachment to a poetical pedigree which has become central to modern theatre; from Chekhov's Constantine in *The Seagull* to the willful neurasthenics of Pirandello and Anouilh, our theatre has delighted to cele-brate a certain creative verve in its alienated heroes, whose brooding impertinences can be traced to the latest Woody Allen concoction in our cinema."

■

Don't Trifle with Love is unusually eclectic in style even for the whimsical Musset. It was composed in two stages. He made a false start in verse on the opening scene, then apparently went right on to begin his prose version, getting through all but the last scene of Act Two before embarking on his trau-matic trip to Italy with Sand. He didn't go back to the play until he was in Paris again. Resuming work, he incorporated a passage from a letter that Sand had just written him. (This is Perdican's paean to love as the only self-validation; it closes Act Two.) Then he wrote straight on to the despairing dénouement. This account of the composition of *Don't Trifle* seems consistent with the play's inconsistencies. The language of the Chorus is less heightened after Act Two. And the anticlerical satire drops off considerably in favor of the young people's struggle to cope with their fear, their pride and their love for each other.

Musset sometimes copied his writings in his life. It's difficult, for example, to read the last line of *André del Sarto* (1833), in which del Sarto, dying, says that now his wife is free to marry his best friend, without thinking of the author's departing gesture in Venice (1834) when he put Sand's hand in Pagello's. But Musset *often* copied his life in his writings. It's impossible to read the last act of *Don't Trifle* and not think of the romantic calamity he'd just undergone.

Might we imagine that Musset began the play with a happy conclusion in mind? The title seems to suggest that he didn't. *On ne badine pas avec l'amour* is an injunction—"One mustn't trifle with love"; but it's also an admonition—"One *can't* trifle with love; if you try, it will revenge itself in earnest." But another fact about the title reopens the speculation. When Musset started the play, he was calling it *Camille et Perdican*.

The play premiered, at the Comédie-Française, in 1861. This time most of the revision was the result of censorship. The clerics became *secular* buffoons and the grim picture of the convent was softened. The play did well and it is now established as Musset's most-performed work. In 1923, the Comédie changed over to the original text, and that is what every French schoolchild reads today at about the age when American children read *Julius Caesar*.

The contrast in presentation between the *fantoches* of *Don't Trifle* and its hero and heroine is even sharper than in most

Musset. A 1968 production by the Tréteau de Paris made the *fantoches* literally two-dimensional by projecting them as cartoons on the back wall of the set.

Nagle Jackson prepared his translation for his own production at the McCarter Theatre in Princeton, New Jersey. He states: "I still find it one of the most radical and truly shocking stage pieces around, cloaked in a *comédie-pastorale* setting. It is the only play I know that has a spiritual rape in it (unless you count Hamlet and Ophelia). Is it a comedy? No. Is it a tragedy? Well, sort of, in a contemporary sense. I find it absolutely fascinating. After Brecht, Beckett and Ionesco we don't need, or even want, a tidy flow of dramatic action leading to the obligatory scene and purgative climax. We like to be jerked around a bit, and Musset was doing that a hundred and fifty years ago."

■

Lorenzaccio was published in August, 1834. When it was written is problematic. Until the 1950s, scholars believed that Musset's travels in Italy and the last agonies of his affair with Sand were necessary background for the setting and the black pessimism of this huge work, which must therefore have been composed after his return alone to Paris. But the discovery of a letter from Musset to his publisher suggests that he wrote the play before leaving Paris for Italy.

The play's ultimate source was Benedetto Varchi's *History of Florence*. Musset used this work directly. But he also consulted, and may have been directed to the subject by, a sketchy, perhaps unfinished composition by Sand that was itself based on Varchi. This unpublished work, which Sand gave to Musset for his use, was titled *Une Conspiracion en 1537*. It belonged to a short-lived Romantic genre called the *scène historique*. Romantic writing, according to one of its proponents, Louis Reybaud, "was to sing with the bird, whiten with the wave, grow green with the leaf." In that spirit, the *scène historique* purported to convey history unedited and un-editorialized, presenting events in their factual sequence, imposing no dramatic structure. Sand arranged (or rather refrained from arranging) six episodes in the preparation and accomplishment by Lorenzo de Medici of his assassination of Alessandro, the corrupt Duke of Florence. Five of the thirty-eight scenes in Musset's massive drama correspond to scenes in *Une Conspiracion*. Some of Musset's characterization and language also seems to stem from the *scène*. However, Musset corrected some misreadings Sand had made (including the date of the events, which actually took place in 1536); and, of course, the great bulk of his material had no basis in the sketch.

Musset portrays three different plots against Alessandro. Lorenzo and the patriot Philip Strozzi want to kill him; the Marquise Ricciarda Cibo, who becomes his mistress, wants to reform him. Most playwrights would have interwoven these three lines of action. Musset keeps them virtually independent—in the case of Ricciarda, completely independent. One of his themes, after all, is human isolation. The suffering city of the play has nearly come apart.

The play's narrative looseness, however compensated for by its dense thematic weave, has combined with its great length (*Lorenzaccio* is nearly twice as long as Musset's second-longest play) in tempting producers to adapt it. It was first produced in 1896; Sarah Bernhardt played Lorenzo. The version she commissioned for the occasion was a hatchet job that reduced the play to a spectacular star turn. Subsequent adaptations have been more balanced (though Paul Thompson's 1977 version for the Royal Shakespeare Company, a Marxist reworking with Brechtian songs, was out of balance in a different way) but the casting of a woman in the lead has remained a frequent choice. As recently as the 1970s, Pat Galloway performed the role at Stratford, Canada. A woman as Lorenzo may have made audiences less uncomfortable with the strong suggestion of a sexual relationship between the assassin and his victim. Gérard Philipe was a famous Lorenzo (and Perdican, and Octave in *Marianne*) at the Théâtre National Populaire.

Paul Schmidt wrote his version of the play for the American National Theater in Washington, D.C. on a commission from Peter Sellars. It is, of course, shortened, but the original's proportions are preserved. Schmidt states that he has avoided nineteenth-century diction in his English. "That belongs to another era. I tried to find language that would ring right, today, to an American ear. Musset's is a difficult tradition for the English-language theatre. Producers try to assimilate his texts, and Marivaux's, to English Restoration comedy. They make it camp." Schmidt calls the play a "penetrating story of a political corruption. It's very relevant to America today."

■

You Can't Think of Everything (*On ne saurait penser à tout*) was written in 1849 for a charity matinee. It quickly went into the repertoire of the Comédie-Française, where it has remained to this day. The play is what Musset called an *imitation* of Louis Carmontelle's sketch *The Scatterbrain* (*Le Distrait*), which dates from the previous century. When Musset published his collected plays he called the volumes *Comédies et proverbes*. Not all his plays with proverbial titles are *proverbes*. (*The Cup and the Lip* and *Don't Trifle with Love* are not.) *You Can't Think*, however, is, and it represents the genre well.

In the eighteenth century, there developed a market for

short pieces whose last line was a proverb. The game was to guess the proverb during the course of the performance. These sketches were published as pamphlets and sold to families who performed them in their parlors. Eventually, professionals started using *proverbes* as curtain-raisers. That's how the Comédie-Française now uses *A Door Should Be Either Open or Shut*, *Don't Take an Oath on Anything* (*Il ne faut jurer de rien*), and *You Can't Think of Everything*.

Michael Feingold did his translation for a book of post-Molière French comedy he was assembling with the support of a National Endowment for the Arts grant. He states: "In *Lorenzaccio* and *Don't Trifle with Love*, Musset painted in oil with big strokes. The *proverbes* are watercolors painted with feather strokes. They're valid theatre, but for intimate audiences. He holds a human interaction, a personality, himself—he could laugh at himself—up to the light and turns it to show its facets. A piece like *You Can't Think of Everything* is about turns in the dialogue, the gradations as you go from one state of feeling to the next. It's all nuance."

—*Amlin Gray*

Fantasio

TRANSLATED BY
RICHARD HOWARD

The King of Bavaria

The Prince of Mantua

Marinoni, his aide-de-camp

Rutten, the King's secretary

Fantasio
Spark
Hartman } young men about town
Facio

Elsbeth, the King's daughter

Her Governess

Officers, pallbearers, tailor, pages, etc.

Munich.

Act One

SCENE ONE

The court. The King, surrounded by courtiers, Rutten.

KING: My friends, some time has passed since I informed you of my dear Elsbeth's engagement to the Prince of Mantua. It is now my duty to inform you of this Prince's arrival; perhaps tonight—tomorrow at the latest—he will be in this palace. It is my wish that the occasion be one of general rejoicing—let the prisons be opened, and let the people spend the night as they would a festival. Rutten, where is my daughter?

The courtiers withdraw.

RUTTEN: Sire, she is in the palace gardens with her governess.

KING: I have not yet seen her today. Why should this be? Is it because she is saddened by her approaching marriage, or perhaps because she is so glad of it?

RUTTEN: Sire, it is my impression that the Princess's face

was shadowed by a certain melancholy. What young woman is not pensive on the eve of her wedding? And she has been upset by St. John's death.

KING: She has? The death of a half-blind hunchback court jester has upset the Princess Elsbeth?

RUTTEN: Sire, the Princess loved him.

KING: Tell me, Rutten, you have had occasion to observe this Prince; what manner of man is he? Here I am, bestowing upon him what I hold dearest in all the world, yet I do not even know him!

RUTTEN: Sire, my stay in Mantua was extremely brief.

KING: You may speak freely, Rutten. With whose eyes can I see the truth if not with yours?

RUTTEN: Truly, sire, I can tell you nothing of the noble Prince's mind and character.

KING: Has it come to this? You hesitate—you, a courtier? How full the air of this room would be of hyperboles and flattering metaphors, had you found this Prince, who tomorrow will be my son-in-law, worthy of such a title. Could I have been mistaken, my friend? Have I made a bad choice?

RUTTEN: Sire, the Prince is said to be the best of monarchs.

KING: Politics, what a spider web! In which we poor mutilated flies struggle so helplessly. My daughter's happiness must not be sacrificed to dynastic concern . . .

They exit.

SCENE TWO

A street. Spark, Hartman and Facio, drinking around a table.

HARTMAN: After all, a princess doesn't get married every
day. Let's drink and smoke and see how much noise
we can make.

FACIO: Why not join the crowd and squash a few Chinese
lanterns over the heads of some respectable citizens?

SPARK: Why not just sit here and smoke in peace?

HARTMAN: Who wants to do anything *in peace*? If I had to
be a clapper hanging in the church bell, I'd still ring
in the holidays. Where the devil is Fantasio?

SPARK: Let's not do anything until he comes.

FACIO: Oh, he'll find us eventually. He's probably getting
drunk in some hole in the wall. Hey! another round
here! *(Raises his glass)*

An officer enters.

OFFICER: Gentlemen, it is my duty to request that you go
elsewhere if you wish to continue your . . . celebration.

HARTMAN: Why the devil should we?

OFFICER: Gentlemen, at this very moment the Princess is
on that terrace over there, and you can readily
understand that she should not be disturbed by your
noisemaking.

FACIO: This is insufferable!

SPARK: What's the difference if we drink here or
somewhere else?

HARTMAN: Who knows if we'll be allowed to drink
somewhere else? Just wait and see: some fool in a green
uniform will crawl out from under every cobblestone

in town *to request that we continue our celebrations* . . . on the moon!

Enter Marinoni, wearing a cloak.

SPARK: The Princess has never issued an order in her life. God save the Princess! If she doesn't want to hear us laughing, she must be sad—or maybe she's going to sing. Let's leave her in peace.

FACIO: Aha! Over there's some foreigner in a cloak nosing for news. He looks like he wants to talk to us.

MARINONI *(Approaching)*: I'm a stranger here, gentlemen. What is the occasion of these observances?

SPARK: Our Princess Elsbeth is getting married.

MARINONI: Ah, a fine figure of a woman, I presume?

HARTMAN: About as fine a figure as you are, sir.

MARINONI: And beloved by her people, to judge from the way the whole town is illuminated?

HARTMAN: Right you are, sir, all these Chinese lanterns, as you have so observantly . . . observed, are no more and no less than an . . . illumination.

MARINONI: What I meant to ask was whether the Princess is the cause of these signs of festivity?

HARTMAN: The sole cause, O trenchant logician. Were each and every one of *us* to get married, there would be no sign of joy in this ungrateful town.

MARINONI: Happy the princess who succeeds in being loved by her people!

HARTMAN: The light of a few lanterns does not constitute the happiness of a people, dear simpleton. Which need not keep the aforesaid Princess from being as fidgety as a canary.

MARINONI: Indeed? "Fidgety" is the word you said?

HARTMAN: It is, O man of mystery. That is the word I employed.

Marinoni bows and exits.

FACIO: What the devil is that gibbering Italian after? Look at him now, pestering those people over there. I can smell a spy a mile away.

HARTMAN: You can smell nothing of the kind—only his supreme stupidity. That stinks to heaven.

SPARK: Here comes Fantasio.

HARTMAN: What's got into him? He's strutting like a judge. Either I've lost my touch or else he's up to something.

FACIO: Hey, my friend, what'll we do with a night like this on our hands?

FANTASIO *(Entering)*: Anything you say, absolutely anything—except "modern fiction."

FACIO: I say we should mix with this rabble and have ourselves a little fun.

FANTASIO: For which all you need is false noses and fireworks.

HARTMAN: Lift a few wigs, kiss a few girls, smash a few lanterns: assignment settled. Let's get started.

FANTASIO: Once upon a time, there was a king of Persia . . .

HARTMAN: Come on, Fantasio.

FANTASIO: Not me. . . . Count me out.

HARTMAN: Why?

FANTASIO: Let me have a glass of that. *(Drinks)*

HARTMAN: Your cheeks are red as springtime.

FANTASIO: Yes, and my heart is white as winter. My head is like an old chimney—nothing but wind and ashes inside. Whew! *(Sits)* How boring it is when a good time was had by all! If only that heavy sky were one big nightcap and I could pull it over the whole town and every fool in it—right down to the ears. All right, somebody, let's have a joke if you please, a nice old pun or two, something really stale . . .

HARTMAN: Why that?

FANTASIO: So I can laugh. If nothing new makes me laugh anymore, maybe something I know will do the trick.

HARTMAN: I diagnose a touch of melancholia and a tendency to misanthropy.

FANTASIO: All wrong. In fact, I've just come from my mistress.

FACIO: Are you with us or not?

FANTASIO: I'm with you, if you're with me; let's sit here awhile and talk about something really interesting— like our new clothes.

FACIO: Let's not. You may be tired of doing whatever it is you've been doing, but I'm tired of sitting still. I have to get moving, out in the open.

FANTASIO: I suppose you do. I couldn't move if my life depended on it. I just want to sit under these chestnut trees with old Spark here to keep me company. Right, Spark?

SPARK: I guess so.

HARTMAN: In that case, "farewell." We're going to see what's happening to the holiday.

Hartman and Facio exit. Fantasio sits down with Spark.

FANTASIO: As sunsets go, this one's a flop! Nature's not

much of an artist this evening. Just look at that valley over there, will you? Four or five measly clouds crawling up the mountainside—when I was twelve I used to draw landscapes like that on the covers of my schoolbooks.

SPARK: The beer's all right. The tobacco's good!

FANTASIO: You must be sick of me, Spark.

SPARK: No, why should I be?

FANTASIO: Because I'm so sick of you. Don't you get bored always seeing the same face day after day? What the devil will Hartman and Facio manage to do with this holiday?

SPARK: There's a lot of life in those two—they can't sit still.

FANTASIO: The Arabian Nights—now there's a wonderful thing! O Spark, my dear Spark, why can't you transport me to Persia! Just to get out of my skin for an hour or two—if only I could be someone else, that man over there, for instance!

SPARK: It's not so easy.

FANTASIO: Just look how charming he is, that man over there: those fine silk trousers! those fine red flowers on his waistcoat! that fine watch fob swinging against his belly in counterpoint to those fine coattails fluttering against his fat thighs! I'm convinced he has a thousand ideas in his head that have never occurred to me. Singularity is the very essence of the man! What a pity that everything we say to each other is always the same; the ideas we exchange are just alike in every conversation we have; yet inside each of these isolated machines, what hidden passageways, what secret compartments! Each man bears a whole

world within himself! a world nobody knows that's
born and dies in total silence! What solitudes these
human bodies are!

SPARK: Have a drink, dreamer, and give that brain of
yours a rest.

FANTASIO: You know, there's only one thing that's made
me laugh in the last three days: I owe so much money
to so many people that if I set foot in my own house,
four bailiffs will drag me off to debtors' prison . . .

SPARK: No wonder you're laughing so hard. Where will
you sleep tonight?

FANTASIO: With the first girl who'll have me. Here's how
it is, Spark, my furniture will be auctioned off
tomorrow morning. Let's go bid on some of it, what
do you say?

SPARK: Do you need money, Heinrich? I can lend you
some.

FANTASIO: Idiot, if I didn't have money I wouldn't have
debts. I feel like buying myself a ballet dancer for a
mistress . . .

SPARK: She'd bore you to death.

FANTASIO: No she wouldn't; my imagination would be
filled with pirouettes and white satin toeshoes;
there'd be a glove of mine lying on the balcony
railing from New Year's Day till New Year's Eve, and
I'd be whistling clarinet solos in my dreams, till I
died of guzzling strawberries in my beloved's
beautiful arms. Spark, has it ever occurred to you that
we have nothing to do—no profession, no pursuit . . .

SPARK: Is that what's depressing you?

FANTASIO: Who ever heard of a depressed fencing
master?

SPARK: You don't seem to want to do anything anyway.

FANTASIO: If I didn't want to do anything, Spark, it
would mean I had already done *something*.

SPARK: Well then?

FANTASIO: Well then, what would you have me do? Look
at this smoky old town of ours; there's not a street,
not a square, not an alley I haven't prowled through
thirty times. There's not a cobblestone I haven't
tripped over, not a single house where I don't know
which girl or which old woman is always at the
upstairs window. I can't take one step without walking
in yesterday's footprints. And, my dear friends, this
Munich of ours is nothing compared to my own mind,
where every nook and cranny is a hundred times more
familiar to me. The footpaths of my own fancy are a
hundred times more dilapidated. I've wandered in a
hundred more directions through this tumbledown
cerebellum of mine, where I'm its sole inhabitant;
I've drunk myself stupid in every tavern, wallowing
like an emperor in his golden coach, as well as
trotting like an upright citizen behind his peaceful
mule; and now I dare not enter the place except like a
thief in the night, with a dark lantern in his hand.

SPARK: I don't understand why you keep tormenting
yourself like this. Me for instance, when I smoke, my
thoughts turn into tobacco smoke; when I drink, my
thoughts turn into beer, or champagne if I'm lucky;
when I kiss my mistress's hand, she slides down her
tapering fingers into my very being like an electric
current; all it takes is the fragrance of a flower to
distract me, and the meanest thing in nature is
enough to make me into a bee buzzing into one
pleasure after the next.

FANTASIO: To put it bluntly, you can go fishing.

SPARK: If I enjoy it, I can do anything.

FANTASIO: Even take a bite out of the moon?

SPARK: I wouldn't enjoy that.

FANTASIO: How do you know, Spark? Taking a bite out of the moon isn't to be despised. How about a game of cards?

SPARK: No thanks.

FANTASIO: Why not?

SPARK: Because we'd lose our money.

FANTASIO: God in heaven, what's got into you? Can't you leave that poor mind of yours alone? Do you always have to look on the dark side of things, you imbecile? Lose our money! Have you no heart, no hope, no faith in God? Wretched unbeliever, is that what you are—capable of withering my heart and destroying my illusions, regardless of all my youth and all my joy? *(Begins to dance)*

SPARK: You know, there are times when I can't be sure whether or not you're mad.

FANTASIO *(Still dancing)*: Give me a bell—a glass bell!

SPARK: What for? What do you want a glass bell for?

FANTASIO: Doesn't Jean-Paul say that a man obsessed by a great idea is like a deep-sea diver under a glass bell? Spark, I have no glass bell—no bell at all, and I dance like Jesus on the waves!

SPARK: Why don't you write something, Heinrich— become a writer: that's still the best way to root out your inhumanity and smother your imagination.

FANTASIO: Now if I could just fall in love with a lobster thermidor, or a star sapphire, or even a little seamstress! Spark, let's try building a house, just for the two of us . . .

SPARK: Why don't you write what you dream? That would

make quite an anthology—something that would sell.

FANTASIO: A sonnet's better than an epic, and a glass of wine is best of all. *(Drinks)*

SPARK: Why don't you travel—go to Italy . . .

FANTASIO: I've been to Italy.

SPARK: Well, it's beautiful, Italy—isn't it?

FANTASIO: The mosquitoes are the size of humming-birds, and they bite you all night long.

SPARK: So try France.

FANTASIO: The Rhine wine in Paris tastes like dishwater.

SPARK: England then.

FANTASIO: That's where I am now—do the English have a country? I'd just as soon see them here as where they live.

SPARK: Then go to the devil!

FANTASIO: If only there was a devil in heaven! If only there was a hell, I'd blow my brains out to reach it! What a wretched thing is man—why he can't even jump out a window without breaking his legs! Imagine having to play the violin ten years to be a decent musician! You have to study to be a painter, to be a stableboy, to make an omelette! Listen, Spark, sometimes I want to sit on a parapet and watch the river flow past and begin counting, one, two, three, four, five, six, seven, and so on until the day I die.

SPARK: Most people would find what you're saying pretty funny, Fantasio, but I think it's awful—the history of our times. Eternity is one big aerie out of which the centuries soar like so many eaglets, one after the next across the sky, and disappear; now it's our turn to wait for death while we watch the sky we can't even get ourselves into . . .

FANTASIO *(Singing)*:

> O change "my life" into "my soul"!
>
> Which, like my love, exists forever

That's Byron, Spark, from the Portuguese. Have you ever heard a prettier refrain? I never think of it without wanting to love someone.

SPARK: Like whom?

FANTASIO: Whom? I haven't a clue: some plump little maid like the ones in Franz Hals; someone soft as the west wind, someone pale as moonlight; someone sad as the servant girl in Flemish paintings who hands a stirrup cup to a traveler in tall boots, sitting straight as a ramrod on his big white horse. Spark, can you see how wonderful that stirrup cup is! Can you see that girl on her doorstep, with the firelight glowing behind her, the supper cooking and the children in bed; all the peace of country life in that one corner of the painting, and the man still breathing hard, but sitting firm in the saddle after riding twenty leagues, and thirty still to go, then one swig of brandy, and goodbye! How dark the night out there, how deep the woods, and how dangerous the weather. . . . The girl stares after him a minute, then as she turns back to the fire, she offers up that sublime charity of the poor as she murmurs: may God protect him!

SPARK: If you were in love, Heinrich, you'd be the happiest man on earth.

FANTASIO: Love no longer exists, my dear friend. Religion, its old nurse, has withered breasts like an old purse with one copper penny inside. Love is the wafer the two of you must break in half at the altar and swallow together in a kiss—there's no altar now, and no love. Hurrah for nature, Spark, we still have wine. *(Drinks)*

SPARK: You'll be drunk.

FANTASIO: You're right. I'll be drunk.

SPARK: It's a little late for that.

FANTASIO: What do you call late? Is noon late? Is midnight early? Where do you start your day? Enough of that, Spark, if you please. Let's drink, let's talk, even if it's only politics or philosophy, or better still nonsense; let's think up ideal governments—or what do you say we catch all the moths that fly over this candle and put them in our pockets. Tell me, Spark, what do you think of steam cannons as a philanthropic invention?

SPARK: I don't follow.

FANTASIO: Once upon a time there was a king who was very, very wise, and very, very happy . . .

SPARK: And then?

FANTASIO: The one thing missing in all his happiness was . . . children. So he prostrated himself in every mosque . . .

SPARK: What are you driving at?

FANTASIO: I'm thinking of my beloved Arabian Nights. That's the way they all begin. Listen, Spark, I'm drunk. I've got to do something. *(Sings)* La la, la la la, la la. . . . All right, let's get up!

A hearse passes.

Hey there, good souls, who're you burying now? This is no time for a funeral.

PALLBEARERS: We're burying St. John.

FANTASIO: St. John is dead? The King's jester is dead? Who's taken his place—the Minister of Justice?

PALLBEARERS: No one's taken his place—you can take it yourself, if you want it. *(They exit)*

SPARK: You deserved that. What can you expect but insolence if you talk to such people?

FANTASIO: There was nothing insolent about it. The fellow was merely giving me some friendly advice, which as it happens I'm taking to heart here and now.

SPARK: You're going to be the court jester?

FANTASIO: This very night, if they'll have me. Since I can't sleep at home, why not attend the royal farce that's being put on tomorrow—and in the royal box!

SPARK: Inspired! You'll be recognized and thrown out by the palace guard first thing. Aren't you some sort of—aren't you the late Queen's godson?

FANTASIO: I won't be that stupid. I'll get myself a hump and a red wig, just like St. John, and no one will know me—not if I have fifty godmothers on my heels. *(Knocks at a door)* Hey, my good man, open up if you're still in there, you and your wife and all your brats!

TAILOR *(Opening the shop door)*: What is it Your Lordship requires?

FANTASIO: You're the court tailor, aren't you? *(Reading the shop sign)* . . . By appointment to His Majesty . . .

TAILOR: At your service, sir.

FANTASIO: So you're the one who made St. John's suits for him?

TAILOR: Indeed I am, sir.

FANTASIO: Then you must have known him. You knew which side he wore his hump on, and how he curled his moustache, and just the color of his wig . . . ?

TAILOR *(Giggling uneasily)*: The gentleman will have his
little joke.

FANTASIO: Fellow, I've never been more serious in my
life. Get back into your shop, and if you don't want to
find some arsenic in your morning coffee, you'll
button your lip about what's going to happen there.

Exits with the tailor. Spark follows them.

SCENE THREE

*An inn on the Munich road. Enter the Prince of Mantua and
Marinoni.*

PRINCE: Well, colonel?

MARINONI: Your Highness?

PRINCE: Well, Marinoni?

MARINONI *(Reading his notes)*: "Melancholy, fidgety,
hysterical, utterly obedient to her father, very fond of
parsnips."

PRINCE: Write that down. And watch what you're doing.
You know I can't read anything but capital letters.

MARINONI *(Writing)*: Me-lan-cho . . .

PRINCE: Write in a whisper; ever since dinner I've been
considering an important scheme.

MARINONI: Here is what Your Highness requested.

PRINCE *(Reading)*: Very good. From now on you're my
intimate friend. By royal appointment. There's no
finer handwriting in all my kingdom. Sit down there.
At a certain distance. Now, my friend, you believe you
have secretly discovered the character of the Princess,
my future bride?

MARINONI: Yes, Your Highness, I have repeatedly
frequented the vicinity of the palace, and these notes
contain the principal features of the various
conversations in which I participated.

PRINCE *(Looking at himself in a pocket mirror)*: I believe I
am curled and oiled as the veriest varlet.

MARINONI: The garments are splendid.

PRINCE: What would you say, Marinoni, were you to see
your master wearing a plain olive-drab frock coat
with no more than a single ribbon in the lapel?

MARINONI: Your Highness chooses to mock my credulity.

PRINCE: No, colonel. You must learn that your master is
the most romantical of men.

MARINONI: "Romantical," Your Highness?

PRINCE: Yes, my friend (I have bestowed this title upon
you). The important scheme I have been pondering is
undreamed of in my family. I intend to arrive at the
court of my future father-in-law in the apparel of a
simple aide-de-camp. It is not sufficient to have sent
a member of my staff to collect gossip concerning the
future Princess of Mantua (that member, Marinoni,
being yourself)—I wish to conduct further
observations with My Own Eyes.

MARINONI: Can this be true, Your Highness?

PRINCE: You must not be petrified. A man like myself
must have as his intimate friend one who is
enterprising of mind and daring in action.

MARINONI: Only one thing appears to me likely to
frustrate Your Highness's scheme.

PRINCE: And what might that be?

MARINONI: The notion of such a disguise could only
belong to the glorious Prince who governs us. But if
my gracious sovereign is secreted among the general

staff, whom will the King of Bavaria honor with the splendid banquet to be given in the Grand Gallery?

PRINCE: A good point, my friend: if I am to be in disguise, then my place must be taken by someone else. Which is impossible, Marinoni—I had not thought of that.

MARINONI: Why impossible, Your Highness?

PRINCE: Of course I am capable of lowering princely dignity to the rank of colonel, but you can scarcely suppose I can consent to elevating an ordinary person to my own level? Moreover, do you suppose that my future father-in-law would forgive such a transgression?

MARINONI: The King of Bavaria is said to be a man of sense and discernment, with an amiable disposition.

PRINCE: It is only with the greatest reluctance, colonel, that I renounce my scheme! Ah, without ceremony and without calling attention to myself, to penetrate this new court, to approach the Princess under a false name, and perhaps even to win her love!—Oh, I digress; such things are surely impossible. . . . Marinoni, my friend, you must try on my dress uniform—I cannot resist the temptation!

MARINONI *(Bowing)*: Your Highness!

PRINCE: Do you suppose that future centuries will forget such an unparalleled episode?

MARINONI: Never, gracious Prince.

PRINCE: Then come and try on my coat.

They exit.

Act Two

SCENE ONE

The palace gardens of the King of Bavaria. Enter Elsbeth and her governess.

GOVERNESS: My poor eyes have wept, my dear—streams of heavenly tears.

ELSBETH: How kind you are! I loved St. John too. He was so witty, and so discreet—he was no ordinary jester, was he?

GOVERNESS: To think that the poor man has left us on the eve of your betrothal! He who spoke of you and you alone on every occasion, day in, day out. Such a merry fellow he was, and so clever that he made you love his very ugliness, you couldn't take your eyes off him in spite of yourself.

ELSBETH: Don't mention my betrothal, it's just one more calamity.

GOVERNESS: But haven't you heard that the Prince of Mantua is arriving today? They say he's a real Amadis . . .

ELSBETH: You're talking nonsense, my dear! According to everything I've heard, he's incredibly hideous and stupid. The whole country knows all about him.

GOVERNESS: Really! I was told he's a real Amadis.

ELSBETH: I'm not asking for an Amadis, my dear, but sometimes being a king's daughter is a cruel fate. My father is the kindest of men; the marriage he has arranged will insure our country's peace, and in return he will receive his people's blessing; I, alas, will have only his, and nothing more.

GOVERNESS: How miserable you sound!

ELSBETH: If I were to refuse the Prince, war would soon begin all over again; how dreadful that these peace treaties must always be signed with tears! I'd like to be a "sensible girl" and resign myself to marrying the first man to come along, if it is a political necessity. Being a nation's mother is a consolation to true hearts, but not to weak wills. You know what a dreamer I am, my dear—perhaps your novels are to blame; you always have one with you somewhere . . .

GOVERNESS: Lord! Please don't tell a soul!

ELSBETH: I know so little about life, and I've dreamed so much.

GOVERNESS: If the Prince of Mantua were as you describe him, God would not let this marriage come to pass, I'm convinced of that.

ELSBETH: Don't be absurd, my dear. God lets men do as they like, and He pays no more heed to our complaints than to the bleating of lambs.

GOVERNESS: I'm certain that if you were to refuse the Prince, your dear father wouldn't force you to marry him.

ELSBETH: No, of course he wouldn't. Which is just why I

must make the sacrifice. Do you think I could ask my
father to revoke his word and with a stroke of the pen
cancel his honorable name on a document which will
bring happiness to millions? What does one unhappy
girl matter! I must enable my father to be a good king.

GOVERNESS: Oh my dear! *(Weeps)*

ELSBETH: Don't weep over me, my dear, you'll only make
me weep as well, and a royal fiancée must not have
red eyes. Don't trouble yourself over the matter any
longer. After all, I shall be a queen, and that may be
. . . amusing. Perhaps I shall develop an interest in my
new clothes—who knows, even in my new carriages,
and my new court as well; fortunately there's more to
a princess's marriage than a husband. Perhaps I'll
find happiness among my wedding gifts.

GOVERNESS: You're truly a Paschal lamb.

ELSBETH: Now my dear, let's begin with a smile or two,
and save our tears for when we may need them. They
say that the Prince of Mantua is the most ridiculous
thing you ever saw.

GOVERNESS: If only St. John were here!

ELSBETH: Oh, St. John . . . St. John!

GOVERNESS: You loved him very much, my dear.

ELSBETH: It was so strange; his wit bound me to him
with invisible threads which seemed to start in my
own heart; his constant mockery of my romantic
notions pleased me immoderately, whereas I find it
painful to endure people who feel as I do; I don't
know what it was about him, something in his eyes, in
his gestures, in the way he took a pinch of snuff. . . .
What a curious fellow he was; whenever he spoke to
me, I would see enchanting scenes—his words

brought the most wonderful things to life, as though by a magic spell.

GOVERNESS: A real Triboulet, that's what he was.

ELSBETH: I don't know about that, but he was a jewel among jesters.

GOVERNESS: Those pages keep going in and out over there; I imagine that the Prince will be making his appearance before long. We must return to the palace and get you dressed.

ELSBETH: I beg you to leave me here for just a quarter of an hour longer; go get my things ready. Unfortunately, my dear, I haven't much longer for dreaming.

GOVERNESS: Lord, is it possible this marriage will take place if it is against Your will? Is it possible for a father to sacrifice his daughter? Will the King turn out to be a veritable Jepthah?

ELSBETH: Don't speak ill of my father, my dear. Go and get ready what I will need.

The governess leaves.

There seems to be someone over there behind those bushes. Can it be the ghost of my poor jester that I see among those cornflowers, sitting on the ground? Who are you? Answer me! What are you doing here, picking those flowers? *(She walks toward a flower bed)*

FANTASIO *(Sitting on the ground, wearing motley, with a hunchback and a wig)*: Who am I? Merely a decent flower picker, who wishes your lovely eyes well.

ELSBETH: What kind of travesty is this costume? Why do you mock someone I loved by wearing that absurd wig? Are you some sort of jester's apprentice?

FANTASIO: May it please Your Serene Highness, I'm the King's new jester; the major-domo has approved my application, I have been introduced to the groom of the bedchamber, the scullions took me under their wing last night, and here I am, modestly picking flowers until I find some wit.

ELSBETH: The one flower I very much doubt you can pick.

FANTASIO: Why not? An old man can find wit just as readily as a young girl. How difficult it is, sometimes, to know if you're twinkling or twaddling. The main thing is to keep talking—the worst marksman in the world can hit the bullseye if he fires 780 bullets a minute, just as easily as a crack shot who fires only once or twice. All I ask is to be fed sufficiently to sustain my stomach in its preferential shape, and I'll keep my eye on my shadow to see if my wig is growing.

ELSBETH: So here you are, wearing St. John's old clothes. . . . Talk about your shadow—as long as you wear his motley, it will always look more like his than yours!

FANTASIO: Just now I was composing an elegy that will decide my fate.

ELSBETH: What kind of fate can be decided?

FANTASIO: My verses will prove either that I'm the world's greatest poet, or else that I have no talent whatever. I'm moving heaven and earth to fit them into an acrostic. The sun, moon and stars are fighting to get into my rhymes, like schoolboys lining up for the circus.

ELSBETH: Poor fool! What a trade you've chosen! grinding out wit at so much per hour. . . . What's wrong with your arms and legs—wouldn't you do better digging up the ground than your own brain?

FANTASIO: Poor lady! What a trade you've chosen! marrying a dolt you've never laid eyes on. . . . What's wrong with your heart and head—wouldn't you do better selling your gowns than your body?

ELSBETH: You have a lot of nerve, for a newcomer, sir.

FANTASIO: What's the name of this flower, if you please?

ELSBETH: A tulip. What does it matter?

FANTASIO: A red tulip, or a blue one?

ELSBETH: Blue, I should say.

FANTASIO: Nothing of the kind—it's a red tulip, as any fool can see.

ELSBETH: That's pretty old news for such a new fool: you don't need wit to tell me there's no disputing tastes . . .

FANTASIO: I'm not disputing; I'm telling you this is a red tulip, even though I admit it's a blue one.

ELSBETH: How do you manage that?

FANTASIO: It's like your marriage contract: who in this world can say if he's born blue or red? Even the tulips don't know. Gardeners and lawyers make such amazing grafts that apples turn to pumpkins, and thistles emerge from the jawbone of an ass to float in mustard on a bishop's silver plate. Now this tulip here may have had expectations of being red, but they married her off; she's amazed to find herself blue: that's how the whole world gets transformed by human hands. Even Mother Nature must have to laugh at herself sometimes, when she glimpses that eternal masquerade in her lakes and ponds. Do you think the Garden of Eden smelled of roses? No, only of new-mown hay. Your rose is the daughter of civilization—your rose is a marquise, like you and me.

ELSBETH: The hawthorn's pale blossom might become a rose, and a thistle can turn into an artichoke, but one flower can't change into another, so what does Mother Nature care? We don't change nature, we adorn or destroy her. The sickliest violet would rather die than succumb to all your devices to change a single stamen.

FANTASIO: That's why I value a violet more than a king's daughter.

ELSBETH: There are some things even a jester isn't entitled to make fun of. Be careful what you say. If you were eavesdropping on what I was telling my governess, look out for your ears!

FANTASIO: Not for my ears, my tongue! You've got the wrong sense, my lady.

ELSBETH: If you want to earn your livelihood, spare me your puns; and if you don't want to earn something else, spare me your botanical comparisons.

FANTASIO: Who knows? Your pun can be a great consolation, and a play on words is sometimes a fine way to play with thoughts, or actions, or even persons. Everything's a pun in this world, and it's as hard to understand the stare of a four-year-old child as the gibberish of three modern plays.

ELSBETH: You must see the world through a changing prism.

FANTASIO: We all have our eyeglasses, but nobody knows just what color his lenses are. How can I ever tell if I'm really happy or wretched, good or bad, stupid or witty?

ELSBETH: You're really ugly, that's for certain.

FANTASIO: No more certain than your beauty, my lady. Here comes your father with your future husband.

Who can tell if you'll marry him or not? *(Exits)*

ELSBETH: Since I can't avoid meeting the Prince of
Mantua, I might as well get it over with.

*Enter the King, Marinoni dressed as the Prince, and the
Prince, dressed as his own aide.*

KING: Prince, this is my daughter. Be so good as to
forgive the simplicity of her attire. You are the guest
of one bourgeois who governs others, and our
protocol is as indulgent of ourselves as of them.

MARINONI: Allow me to kiss this charming hand,
madame, if that is not granting an excessive favor to
these lips.

ELSBETH: Your Highness will excuse me if I return to the
palace. I trust we shall enjoy a more suitable meeting
at the reception ceremony this evening. *(Exits)*

PRINCE: The Princess is entirely correct. Now that is
what I should call a divine modesty.

KING *(To Marinoni)*: Just who is this aide-de-camp that
follows you about like your shadow? I find it
intolerable, the way he keeps adding some inept
remark to whatever we say. Be so good as to dismiss
him.

Marinoni whispers to the Prince.

PRINCE *(Also whispering)*: Very clever of you to have
persuaded him to dismiss me; I shall attempt to join
the Princess and drop a few hints in her ear—ever so
subtly, you know. *(Exits)*

KING: That aide-de-camp of yours is an idiot, my friend.
How can you bear the fellow?

MARINONI: Hmm! Hmm! Let us stroll a bit farther, if
Your Majesty will be so kind; I believe I glimpsed a
charming kiosk in the shrubbery over there.

They exit.

SCENE TWO

An anteroom in the palace. Fantasio lying on the carpet.

FANTASIO: What a life, being a jester! I may have been
drunk yesterday, when I put on the motley and turned
up at the palace; but to tell the truth, I never had a
better idea when I was sober than this crazy business.
I appear, and here I am, settled in, pampered and
petted, registered on the payroll, and best of all,
forgotten! I come and go in the palace as if I had
lived here all my life. Just now I ran into the King; he
didn't even have the curiosity to look at me; now that
his jester's dead, they must have told him, "Sire,
here's a new one." Wonderful! At last, God be
thanked, my mind is at rest, I can talk all the
nonsense I please without anyone's doing anything to
stop me; I'm one of the household pets of the King
of Bavaria, and so long as I hold onto my hump and
my wig, I can live here until the day I die, somewhere
between a spaniel and a parakeet. Meanwhile, my
creditors can batter my door down for all I care. I'm
as safe here, under this wig, as I would be in the
West Indies . . .

Isn't that the Princess I see there in the next room,
through this grating? Yes, there she is, trying on her

wedding veil, with two long tears running down her cheeks; now one falls, like a pearl, onto her bosom. Poor little thing! I *did* overhear what she and her governess were saying this morning, even though it was an accident. I was sitting there among the flowers with nothing more on my mind than taking a nap. And now there she is, crying away, with no suspicion that I'm watching her again. If only I were still a schoolboy, how deeply would I reflect upon the wretchedness of royalty, upon this lamb with a pink ribbon round her neck by which to lead her all the more readily to the shambles! The child is probably romantically minded and finds it a cruel fate to have to marry a man she's never met. Yet she sacrifices herself in silence. How strange is fate! Here I have to get drunk, and encounter St. John's funeral procession, and put on his motley, and take his place in the palace—in other words, commit the wildest folly in the world, all in order to look through that grille and see the only two tears the girl may ever weep on her wretched wedding veil. *(Exits)*

SCENE THREE

A path in the garden, the Prince, Marinoni.

PRINCE: Colonel, you are a fool and nothing but a fool.
MARINONI: Your Highness is most painfully mistaken in my regard.
PRINCE: You are not merely a fool, you are a lout, a churl and a clod! Couldn't you have prevented it? I entrust you with the greatest scheme to be devised in countless ages and you, my best friend, my loyal

servant, can do nothing but add one blunder to the next. No, no—whatever you say, your conduct is unforgivable!

MARINONI: How could I keep Your Highness from suffering the unfortunate consequences of the role you had determined to take? You order me to assume your name and to conduct myself as the true Prince of Mantua. Can I prevent the King of Bavaria from offering an insult to my aide-de-camp? You were entirely mistaken to concern yourself with our conversation.

PRINCE: First of all, an oaf of your stripe has no business giving me orders.

MARINONI: Consider, Your Highness, that I must be either the Prince or his aide-de-camp. Whether one or the other, I act only on your orders.

PRINCE: Calling me "impertinent" in front of the entire court because I wished to kiss the Princess's hand!

MARINONI: You must realize, Your Highness, that this unfortunate adjective was addressed to the aide-de-camp and not to the Prince. Do you have any hope of being respected while under that disguise?

PRINCE: Enough. Enough! Give me back my coat.

MARINONI *(Taking off the coat)*: If my sovereign requires, I am prepared to die for him. No sacrifice is too great.

PRINCE: To tell the truth, I cannot make up my mind. On the one hand, I am outraged at what has befallen me, and on the other, I am loath to abandon my scheme. The Princess does not appear indifferent to the secret meanings of the language I have addressed to her. Two or three times already, I have managed to whisper inconceivable things. The matter must be pondered further . . .

MARINONI *(Holding the coat)*: What shall I do, Your
    Highness?

PRINCE: Put it back on, put it on and let us return to the
    palace.

They exit.

SCENE FOUR

Princess Elsbeth, the King.

KING: My daughter, I must have a frank answer to my
    question: do you dislike this marriage?

ELSBETH: The answer, sire, must be your own. If you
    dislike it, I dislike it. If you like it, then I do too.

KING: I find the Prince to be a commonplace person, about
    whom it is difficult to say anything in particular. His
    aide-de-camp's stupidity is the only thing I hold
    against him; he himself may be a good prince, but he
    is not a distinguished man. There is nothing about
    him which attracts or repels me. What can I tell you?
    Women's hearts have secrets impenetrable to me.
    They may create heroes so unusual, and respond so
    singularly to certain aspects of a man they meet, that it
    is impossible to act in their behalf, so long as one is
    not guided by some tangible clue. Therefore you must
    tell me quite clearly what you think of your fiancé.

ELSBETH: I think that he is the Prince of Mantua, and
    that war will break out again tomorrow between his
    country and ours if I do not marry him.

KING: That is certain, my child.

ELSBETH: Therefore I think that I shall marry him, and

that the war will be over.

KING: May our people's blessings serve as your father's thanks! My beloved daughter, I shall be glad of this alliance; but I should not like to see, in those lovely blue eyes, that sadness which betrays their resignation. Take a few days more in which to reflect.

He exits. Enter Fantasio.

ELSBETH: There you are, poor fellow. Are you enjoying yourself here? What kind of life are you living?

FANTASIO: A life as free as a bird.

ELSBETH: "Like a bird in a cage" would be a better answer. This palace may be a lovely cage, but it is a cage nonetheless.

FANTASIO: The size of a palace or a room does not make a man more or less free. The body moves where it can; the imagination may open wings as wide as the sky in a dungeon the size of a man's hand.

ELSBETH: Then you are a happy fool?

FANTASIO: Very happy. I talk with the puppies in the kennels and the scullions in the kitchens. There is one mongrel, no bigger than this, who has told me the most enchanting things . . .

ELSBETH: In what language?

FANTASIO: In the purest style. He wouldn't make a grammatical mistake from one year to the next.

ELSBETH: Might I hear a few words in that pure style of his?

FANTASIO: As a matter of fact, I'd prefer you didn't. It's a special language—only mongrels can speak it. Trees and cornstalks know it too, but not kings' daughters. When is your wedding?

ELSBETH: In a few days, it will all be over.

FANTASIO: You mean, it will all have begun. I plan to give you a wedding present made by my own hands.

ELSBETH: I'm eager to see what it will be.

FANTASIO: It will be a pretty little stuffed canary, that sings like a nightingale.

ELSBETH: How can it sing if it's stuffed?

FANTASIO: It sings wonderfully.

ELSBETH: You know, there's something fanatical about the way you make fun of me.

FANTASIO: Not at all. My canary has a little whistle in its belly. You touch a little spring under its left foot, and it sings all the new operas, exactly like Mademoiselle Grisi.

ELSBETH: A creation of your own wit, no doubt?

FANTASIO: By no means. It's a court canary; there are a lot of well-brought-up young girls who behave the same way. They have a little spring under their left arm, a pretty little jeweled spring, like a dandy's watch. The tutor or the governess touches the spring, and right away you see their lips produce the prettiest little smile, and a charming stream of honeyed words comes out in the sweetest, gentlest murmur, all very politely, like nymphs dancing on tiptoe round a magic fountain. The bridegroom stares wide-eyed; the audience whispers indulgently, and the father, filled with a secret satisfaction, gazes proudly at his gold shoe buckles.

ELSBETH: You seem to harp on certain subjects. Tell me, jester, what did those poor girls ever do to you, that you should pillory them so mercilessly? Have you no respect for a sense of duty?

FANTASIO: I have a powerful respect for ugliness; that's

why I respect myself so deeply.

ELSBETH: Sometimes you seem to know more than you say. Where are you from? Who are you? In the one day you've been here, you've been able to pluck out the heart of mysteries that princes themselves have never suspected. Is all this folly for my ears alone, or do you speak at random?

FANTASIO: O, at random. I speak entirely at random: random is my dearest confidant.

ELSBETH: And random seems to have taught you what you have no business knowing. I suspect you spy on everything I say or do . . .

FANTASIO: God knows what I do. What do you care?

ELSBETH: I care more than you suppose. Just now, in this very room, while I was trying on my veil, I suddenly heard footsteps behind the arras. If I'm not mistaken, that was you walking there . . .

FANTASIO: Rest assured, Princess, it will remain between your handkerchief and me. I'm no more indiscreet than I am inquisitive. What pleasure could I take in your troubles? And how could your pleasures trouble me? You're one thing, I'm another: lovely and ugly; rich and poor; princess and jester. . . . Need I go on? You can see that there's no connection between us. It's of absolutely no consequence that two wheels, set in different ruts, not even leaving traces in the same dust, should cross the same highway. Is it my fault if one of your tears fell on my cheek while I was sleeping?

ELSBETH: You address me in the shape of a man I cared for—that's why I listen to you in spite of myself. My eyes imagine they're seeing St. John, but perhaps you're nothing but a spy?

FANTASIO: What good would it do me? Suppose it was true that your marriage did cost you a few tears, and I happened to have found it out: what good would it do me to tell someone? I wouldn't be given a penny for the information, nor would you be shut up in a closet somewhere. I understand perfectly that it must be quite tiresome to marry the Prince of Mantua; but after all, I'm not the one who has to do it. Tomorrow or the day after you will have left for Mantua with your wedding gown, and I'll still be here on this stool with these old breeches. Why should I have anything against you? I have no reason to desire your death; you've never loaned me money.

ELSBETH: But if you accidently saw what I want no one to know, should I not get rid of you, lest a subsequent ... accident occurs?

FANTASIO: Are you trying to compare me to a confidant in some tragedy, afraid I'll follow your shadow with declamations? Don't "get rid of me," please. I like it here. Look, there comes your governess, with her pockets full of mysteries. I'll prove that I'm not spying on you—I'll go to the pantry and eat a plover's wing the major-domo has saved for his wife. *(Exits)*

GOVERNESS *(Entering)*: My dear Elsbeth, do you know something terrible?

ELSBETH: What do you mean? You're trembling all over.

GOVERNESS: The Prince is not the Prince, and the aide-de-camp isn't either. It's like a fairy tale.

ELSBETH: What nonsense is this?

GOVERNESS: Sh! Sh! One of the Prince's own officers just told me. The Prince of Mantua is a regular Almaviva; he's in disguise as a member of his own staff! He must have wanted to observe you and get to know you like Haroun-al-Raschid! He's here in disguise, the Prince is in disguise like the Count in *The Barber of Seville*! The man who was introduced to you as your future husband is only an aide-de-camp named Marinoni!

ELSBETH: It can't be true.

GOVERNESS: It is, it is! The real Prince is in disguise: no one can tell who he is; it's a fantastic business!

ELSBETH: And some officer told you this?

GOVERNESS: One of the Prince's officers! You can ask him for yourself . . .

ELSBETH: And he didn't point out the real Prince of Mantua among the aides-de-camp on his staff?

GOVERNESS: Well, you see, he was so frightened, the poor fellow was trembling while he was confiding in me. He only told me his secret because he wants to be nice to you, and he knew I'd warn you. . . . As for that Marinoni, there's no question about who *he* is. The only thing is, I couldn't find out which one is the real Prince . . .

ELSBETH: If it's true, it would certainly be something to think about. All right, bring this officer to me.

Enter a page.

GOVERNESS: What's the matter, Flamel? You're all out of breath.

PAGE: Oh, my lady, it's so funny—only I dare not speak in Your Highness's presence.

ELSBETH: Speak, speak. What's happened?

PAGE: Just when the Prince of Mantua rode into the courtyard, at the head of his whole staff, his wig flew off his head and vanished then and there.

ELSBETH: Well, what of it? How silly!

PAGE: My lady, let me die if it isn't true. The wig flew up
into the air on a hook. We found it in the pantry, next
to a broken bottle. . . . No one knows who played this
trick, but the Prince is absolutely furious, and he
swears that if the culprit isn't caught and *put to death,*
he'll declare war on the King your father and put the
whole country to fire and sword.

ELSBETH: Come listen to the rest of this tale, my dear.
My mood is beginning to change . . .

Enter another page.

Now what—more news?

PAGE: My lady, the King's jester is in prison; he's the one
who pulled off the Prince's wig.

ELSBETH: The jester's in prison? On the Prince's orders?

PAGE: Yes, Your Highness.

ELSBETH: Come with me, my dear, I must speak to you.

Exits with the governess.

SCENE FIVE

The Prince, Marinoni.

PRINCE: No, no, I must reveal myself. It is time for me to
burst upon them. The thing cannot stop here: Fire
and blood! A royal wig on a fishhook? Are we among
barbarians, in the Siberian desert? Is there not still
some vestige of civilization, some rudiment of
decency somewhere under the sun? I seethe with

fury, my eyes are starting out of my head!

MARINONI: You'll ruin everything by this violence.

PRINCE: ... And that father, that King of Bavaria, that monarch so lauded in last year's almanac! that man whose aspect is so seemly, who expresses himself in such measured terms, yet who burst into laughter upon seeing his son-in-law's wig fly up into the air! Yes, I know, Marinoni, I know it was *your* wig that was snatched off your head, but was it still not the wig of the Prince of Mantua, since in you everyone saw the Prince of Mantua? When I think that it might have been myself, in flesh and blood, and that it might have been *my* wig that. ... Ah, there is Providence; when God inspired me with the sudden idea to disguise myself; when the notion flashed upon my brain: "I must mask my person," this fatal event had been foreseen by Destiny. It is Destiny which has rescued from the most intolerable affront the head which rules my people. Yet by heaven all shall be brought out into the light! I shall betray my dignity no longer. Since human and divine majesties are ruthlessly violated, indeed lacerated, since men no longer entertain notions of good and evil, since the King of several thousand subjects burst into laughter like a stableboy at the sight of a wig, Marinoni, give me back my coat!

MARINONI *(Taking off the coat)*: If my sovereign so commands, I am prepared to suffer a thousand tortures for him.

PRINCE: I know your devotion. Come, it is time for me to take appropriate measures with the King.

MARINONI: You reject the Princess's hand? Yet she gazed at you most meaningfully throughout the whole dinner.

PRINCE: She did? You think she did? I am losing my way in a labyrinth of perplexities. Accompany me nonetheless, we shall make our way to the King.

MARINONI *(Holding the coat)*: What must be done, Your Highness?

PRINCE: Put it back on for the nonce. You can return it to me later; they will be only the more petrified to hear me take the appropriate tone, the customary tone of the Prince of Mantua, in this simple frock coat.

They exit.

SCENE SIX

A prison. Fantasio alone.

FANTASIO: I don't know if there's a Providence or not, but it's more amusing to believe there is. Yet here's a poor little princess about to marry against her will a loathsome beast, a provincial booby upon whose head Fortune has dropped a crown the way the eagle dropped a turtle on old Aeschylus. Everything was made ready, sconces were lit, the bridegroom powdered, the poor little bride done with her confession. She had dried the two charming tears I saw her shed this morning. All she lacked was two or three sermons to make her misery complete. And entangled in all this was the fate of two kingdoms and the peace of two peoples; and then I had to be inspired to put on this hump and this motley, to get drunk one more time in our good King's pantry, and then fish out, on the end of a hook and line, the wig of his beloved ally and presumptive son-in-law! To tell the truth, when I'm drunk I believe there's something superhuman about me. Now here's the marriage broken off and everything called into question; the Prince of Mantua demands my head in exchange for his wig; the King of Bavaria finds the punishment somewhat excessive and consents to no more than prison; the Prince of Mantua, God be thanked, is so stupid that he would rather be cut to ribbons than give in; and so the Princess remains a virgin, at least for the time being. If that isn't the subject for an epic poem in twelve cantos, I don't know what is! Boileau and Pope have written glorious verses on far less glorious themes. If only I were a poet, how poetically I would render the scene of that wig soaring through the air. But the man who is capable of doing such things invariably scorns to write them. Thus posterity will have to do without . . .

He falls asleep. Enter Elsbeth and the governess, carrying a lamp.

ELSBETH: He's asleep. Shut the door quietly.

GOVERNESS: Look—there's no doubt about it. He's taken off his wig, the hump has vanished too. There he is, the way his people see him in his triumphal chariot. There he is, the noble Prince of Mantua himself!

ELSBETH: Yes, it is he. And now my curiosity is satisfied. I so wanted to see his face, nothing more. Let me have a good look at him. *(She takes the lamp)* Psyche, watch out for that drop of oil . . .

GOVERNESS: He's as handsome as a young Jesus!

ELSBETH: Why did you give me so many romances and

fairy tales to read? Why did you strew my poor mind
with such strange and mysterious flowers?

GOVERNESS: I can see how moved you are, trembling on
tiptoe there!

ELSBETH: He's waking up. Let's get away.

FANTASIO *(Waking)*: Is this a dream? Am I holding the
hem of a white dress?

ELSBETH: Let go of me! We cannot stay here . . .

FANTASIO: Is it you, Princess? If you're bringing me the
pardon for the King's jester, let me put the hump back
on, and the wig too, it will only take a second . . .

GOVERNESS: Ah! Prince, it ill becomes you to deceive us
so! Do not assume that costume again; we know all.

FANTASIO: Prince! Where do you see a prince?

GOVERNESS: What is the use of pretending now?

FANTASIO: I'm not pretending at all; why on earth are
you calling me Prince?

GOVERNESS: I know my duty to Your Highness.

FANTASIO: My lady, I beg you to explain the words used
by this good woman. Is there truly a vast misunder-
standing, or am I the victim of some sort of joke?

ELSBETH: Why ask, since you yourself are playing the
joke?

FANTASIO: Then am I a prince, by some chance? Has
anyone called my mother's honor into question?

ELSBETH: If you're not the Prince of Mantua, who are
you?

FANTASIO: My name is Fantasio. I am a citizen of
Munich. Here's a letter addressed to me . . .

ELSBETH: A citizen of Munich! Then why are you in
disguise? What are you doing here?

FANTASIO: My lady, I beg your forgiveness. *(Falls to his
knees)*

ELSBETH: What does this mean? Get up, man, and leave this place! I extend you the pardon for a punishment you may well deserve. Who made you do this thing?

FANTASIO: I cannot account for the motive which has brought me here.

ELSBETH: You cannot? You *will* not. And yet I must know it.

FANTASIO: Forgive me, I dare not confess it.

GOVERNESS: Let us go, Elsbeth. Do not expose yourself to language unworthy of you. The man is a thief, or else some upstart who will try to make love to you.

ELSBETH: I must know the reason you have assumed this motley.

FANTASIO: I implore you, spare me.

ELSBETH: No, I shall not. Speak, or this door will close upon you for ten long years.

FANTASIO: My lady, I am riddled with debts; my creditors have obtained a writ against me; at this very moment, my belongings are being sold, and if I were not in this prison, I should be in another. They were to have come and arrested me yesterday evening; not knowing where to spend the night, nor how to escape the bailiffs, I was inspired to assume this motley and to seek refuge at the King's feet; if you restore my freedom, I shall be seized and flung into irons; my uncle is a miser who lives on radishes and potatoes, and who abandons me to die of hunger in every tavern of the realm. Since you insist upon knowing the whole truth, I am in debt for twenty thousand crowns.

ELSBETH: And is all this the truth?

FANTASIO: If I am lying, I promise to pay up.

A noise of horses outside.

GOVERNESS: I hear a carriage passing. It must be the King himself. If I could just signal to a page! *(Calling out the window)* Hey Flamel, is that you? Where are you going?

PAGE *(Outside)*: The Prince of Mantua is leaving.

GOVERNESS: The Prince of Mantua!

PAGE: Yes, war has been declared. There was a terrible scene between him and the King, in front of the whole court, and the Princess's marriage is broken off . . .

ELSBETH: Do you hear that, sir? You are responsible for breaking off my marriage!

GOVERNESS: Lord God above! The Prince of Mantua is leaving, and I never even saw him . . . !

ELSBETH: How terrible that war has been declared!

FANTASIO: Terrible, you say, Your Highness? Would you prefer a husband who makes his wig a matter of life and death? Ah, my lady, if war is declared, we shall know what to do with our arms; the idlers on our street corners will pull on their uniforms; I myself shall take up my old hunting rifle, if it hasn't yet been sold. We shall make a sortie into Italy, and if you ever enter the city of Mantua, it will be as a true queen, without need for any candles but our swords.

ELSBETH: Fantasio. . . . Would you like to stay on as my father's jester? I'll pay the twenty thousand crowns.

FANTASIO: I would, with all my heart. But to tell the truth, if I had to do it, I'd jump out the window to escape, sooner or later.

ELSBETH: Why? You see that St. John is dead; and we

must have a court jester . . .

FANTASIO: As jobs go, I prefer it to any other; but I really can't hold any job. If you think it's worth twenty thousand crowns to be rid of the Prince of Mantua, give them to *me*, and don't pay my debts. A gentleman without debts couldn't show himself in society. . . . It never occurred to me that I might live without debts.

ELSBETH: All right, I'll give you the money. But take the key to my garden as well: the day you're tired of being hounded by your creditors, come and hide in the cornflowers where I found you this morning. Be sure and take your wig and your motley with you; never let me set eyes on you without that fake hump and these silver bells, for that's the way I like you best: you can be my fool again for as long as you like, and then go about your business. You may leave now, you know, the door is open.

GOVERNESS: Is it possible? Can the Prince of Mantua have gone, and I never even saw him?

Don't Trifle With Love

TRANSLATED BY
NAGLE JACKSON

The Baron

Perdican, his son

Master Blazius, an abbot and tutor to Perdican

Master Bridaine, the local curé

Camille, the Baron's niece

Dame Pluche, her governess

Rosette, a village girl, Camille's childhood playmate

Chorus, a village elder

Various peasants, servants, etc.

The mid-eighteenth century.

A country estate and its surroundings.

In the original text, Rosette is Camille's "soeur de lait," that is, the daughter of Camille's wet nurse, sometimes translated as her foster sister. The important point is that she and Camille played together as small children in a sisterlike relationship.

The setting depicts several different areas within and around the Baron's chateau. It is an old country chateau, a working estate. The small village which surrounds it depends upon it as did the feudal peasants who tilled the same land in the Middle Ages. Under the beneficent eye of the Baron, progress and opulence have been successfully avoided. The Chorus is a deliberately poetical invention to set the tone of this deliberately poetical prose play. It is traditionally performed by one or two speakers, silently accompanied by peasants who observe the action.

Act One

SCENE ONE

Before the chateau. The Chorus, an older, silver-haired farmer, gazes offstage. Sitting and standing about are various villagers.

CHORUS: Gingerly rocked on his frisking mule, Master Blazius through the cornflowers comes! Dressed in his best, with writing case a-side, jounced atop his bounding belly like a babe atop a pillow, eyes half-lidded, he mumbles Pater Noster into his triple chins.

Blazius in clerical habit, sitting astride a mule, enters.

Hail, Master Blazius! You arrive at grape-picking time and look like an ancient amphora.

BLAZIUS: Let those who wish to hear news of importance bring me a cool glass of wine.

CHORUS: Here's our most bountiful beaker; drink Master Blazius. The wine is good. You can speak afterwards.

BLAZIUS: Then will you know, my children, that the

Baron's son, young Perdican, has just attained his majority *and* his doctorate from the University of Paris!

They applaud; he drinks.

This very day he returns to the chateau, his mouth so crammed with invention and flowered with figures of speech that most of the time one scarcely knows how to reply!

They applaud; he drinks.

He is a generous book of gold, never sees the slightest blade of grass but nominates its Latin nomenclature, and when it rains, or the tempests rage, he'll tell you exactly *why*. And when you see his illuminations! All done by hand! In several different colors! Your eyes will open wide as that gateway. In fine, he is a perfect diamond, perfect from head to toe, and that is what I've come to tell His Lordship!

They applaud; he drinks.

It must be admitted that some of the glory goes to me, his tutor since he was four, for which reason, good people, bring me a stool and help me down from this fractious beast before I break my neck.

He is carefully unhorsed.

Ahh! And now I wouldn't mind a little pick-me-up before going in.

CHORUS: Drink, Master Blazius, and buck up your spirits.

We were there the day young Perdican was born;
there's no need to go on and on about him. May we
still find a bit of the boy in the heart of the man!

BLAZIUS: Heavens! The cup is dry. Didn't think I'd
drunk so much. . . . Adieu! I have devised, in the
course of my equestrian peregrination, a phrase or
two—entirely without pretension, of course—to
gratify His Lordship's ear. And now, I ring the bell.

*He exits, and we hear the ringing of a porter's bell. Then we
hear a loud and plaintive whinnying from offstage. Dame
Pluche enters, riding on an ass. A groom accompanies her.*

CHORUS: Joltingly jerked on her winded ass, over the
hillock, Dame Pluche, clambering, comes! Her cold
and meager groom, with all his wretched might,
drives on the wretched beast who droops his head,
worrying the thistle in his bit. She spurs him on with
her angry, skinny legs, as with her bony hands she
tells her rosary. Welcome, Dame Pluche! You come to
us like the autumn chill which yellows the forest; you
come to us like the flu.

PLUCHE: Water, you riffraff! A cup of water! With vinegar.

CHORUS: Whence do you come, Pluche my old love? Your
false hair is covered with dust—look! A fallen tuft!
Your chaste skirts have crept up to your sanctified
garters.

PLUCHE: Be advised, peasants, that His Lordship's niece,
the beautiful Camille, comes this day to the chateau.
She has left the convent on strict orders to receive
here the inheritance left her by her mother. Her
education, thanks be to God, is completed, and those

with eyes to see will find in her a perfect flowering of knowledge and devotion. Never has there been such an angel, such a lamb, such a dove of purity as this dear little nun. May God protect and guide her, Amen. Now get out of my way, rabble. My legs are all swollen.

CHORUS *(Handing her a cup of water)*: Tidy yourself, honest Pluche. And when you pray, pray for rain. Our fields are as dry as your old bones.

PLUCHE: This cup smells of the kitchen. Pah! Give me a hand. You are all louts; louts and boobies.

She is dehorsed, and exits in the same direction as Blazius.

CHORUS: Let us put on our Sunday best and wait for the Baron to summon us. Unless I'm way off the mark, there's a feast in the offing today!

SCENE TWO

In the chateau. The Baron's chambers. The Baron, Blazius and Bridaine.

BARON: Master Bridaine, my good friend, allow me to present Master Blazius, tutor to my son. Yesterday, at exactly eight minutes past noon, my son achieved his twenty-first year *and* his doctorate in four disciplines. Master Blazius, allow me to present Master Bridaine, curé of our parish and friend to me.

BLAZIUS: Four disciplines: literature, botany, civil law and canon law.

BARON: Go to your chambers, dear Blazius. My son won't be late in his arrival. Spruce yourself up and come back here when you hear the great bell ringing.

Blazius bows and exits.

BRIDAINE: You know what I think? I think your tutor's had a snootful.

BARON: Impossible!

BRIDAINE: I'd swear to it. He was talking right at me and the smell of wine was enough to pickle your ears.

BARON: Enough I say! I tell you it's impossible.

Pluche enters.

Ah, there you are my good Dame Pluche. My niece is with you?

PLUCHE: She comes in arrears, my lord, which is to say: I precede her.

BARON: Master Bridaine, my good friend, allow me to present Dame Pluche, tutor to my niece. Yesterday at exactly seven o'clock in the evening, she emerged from the finest convent in France. Dame Pluche, allow me to present Master Bridaine, curé of our parish and friend to me.

PLUCHE *(Curtseying)*: The finest convent in France, my lord, and she the finest Christian in it, if I may so expand to Your Lordship.

BARON: Go, Dame Pluche, and pull yourself together. My niece will soon be here, I hope. Be ready when you hear the dinner bell.

Pluche exits.

BRIDAINE: My God, what unction! Most extreme.

BARON: Unction, yes, and compunction. Her virtue is unassailable.

BRIDAINE: But the tutor's had a snootful, that I know for a fact.

BARON: Master Bridaine, there are times when I doubt your friendship. Have you set out to contradict me? Not one word more on that subject. Now, I have drawn up a plan to marry my son to my niece. They're perfectly matched; their educations cost me six thousand crowns.

BRIDAINE: You'll have to get a dispensation.

BARON: I've got it, Bridaine. It's on the table in my study. Oh, my friend, just think how happy I am! You know I've always had a horror of solitude. Nevertheless, my title and the responsibility of office force me to stay in this chateau three months every winter and three each summer. And it's impossible to please everyone in general, and my vassals in particular, without occasionally letting it be known I'm not to be disturbed. How austere, how trying the dignity of office! But what joy will it be to have my son and my daughter-in-law living here, to temper, by their presence, the somber melancholy and bleak austerity which are naturally mine since His Majesty appointed me tax collector.

BRIDAINE: They're gonna get married here or in Paris?

BARON: I thought you'd never ask. Well, well, my friend. . . . *(Taking his hands)* What would you say if these hands of yours, these very hands—well don't look at them as if they were diseased—what if these very hands, I say, were destined to solemnly bless the happy confirmation of my fondest dreams. Eh?

BRIDAINE: I am dumb. Amazement stops my mouth.

BARON: Look! Look out the window. See my people crowding to the gate! My two young ones arrive—at an instant—what a happy coincidence! I've already arranged every move: my niece will be brought in through this doorway on my left, and my son through this one on my right. What do you think? And I shall feast my eyes upon their greeting: to see how they meet, how they react. . . . I don't want any slip-ups. Six thousand crowns is nothing to sneeze at. Anyway the children have been devoted to each other since the cradle. Bridaine! I've got an idea.

BRIDAINE: What?

BARON: During dinner, without making a big thing of it . . . you know, after a couple of drinks—you do know Latin?

BRIDAINE: "*Ita edepol.*" ["Indeed, so!"] Good Lord, of course I do.

BARON: I'd love it if you'd . . . you know . . . try him out. The boy, I mean. Discreetly. In front of his cousin. That could not help but produce a favorable impression. Make him say something in Latin. Maybe not right during dinner, that might be a bit pretentious and besides I wouldn't understand a word, but afterwards. With the dessert. You follow me?

BRIDAINE: Well, if you don't understand a word your niece probably won't either.

BARON: All the more reason. You don't expect a woman to admire something she understands. Where've you been, Bridaine. What pitiful logic.

BRIDAINE: I don't know any women, it's true, but it strikes me peculiar to admire something you can't understand.

BARON: Well, I do know women. I know those charming and inexplicable creatures and I tell you there's nothing they like better than confusion. The more confusion you contrive, the more they'll feed upon, till everything and all is sweet confusion.

Perdican enters, left, and Camille, right.

Greetings, my children. Greetings my dear Camille, my dearest Perdican. Let me embrace you . . . and then embrace each other.

PERDICAN: Greetings, Father. And you, my best beloved coz. What joy. How happy I am.

CAMILLE *(Curtseys demurely)*: My father, my cousin. I salute you both.

PERDICAN: My God, you've grown up, Camille. And lovely . . . lovely as the day.

BARON: When did you leave Paris, Perdican?

PERDICAN: Wednesday. I think. Maybe Tuesday. *(Still gazing at Camille)* Look at this . . . metamorphosis: a woman! So that must mean I'm a man. Seems only yesterday, you were no higher than that.

BARON: You must both be exhausted. A long trip. And such a warm day.

PERDICAN: Heavens, no. Look, Father; Camille is so beautiful.

BARON: Well, then, kiss her. Go kiss your cousin.

Perdican goes to her; she pulls back.

CAMILLE: I must beg your pardon.

PERDICAN: I beg yours.

BARON: Oh, a compliment deserves a kiss. Go on.

PERDICAN: If my cousin demurs when I take her hand, then it is for me to beg pardon. Love steals kisses; not friendship.

CAMILLE: And neither should accept that which they cannot return.

BARON *(To Bridaine)*: Bad news, Bridaine. Bad news and bad beginning.

BRIDAINE *(To Baron)*: Excessive modesty can be a fault, yes, but don't worry: marriage removes a world of scruples.

BARON *(Aside)*: I'm shocked . . . wounded! What kind of a reply is that?: "I must beg your pardon." And she almost made the sign of the cross. I can't stand it. This moment was supposed to make me so happy. I had it all planned . . . Camille at one door, Perdican, the other . . . me in the middle . . . smiling. . . . Ruined! This is terrible. I'm not happy; I'm unhappy!

Camille and Perdican in their embarrassment have begun wandering, separately, about the room.

BRIDAINE *(To Baron)*: Say something to them. They're not even looking at each other.

BARON: Well . . . well, well, well, my children! Thinking about things? What are you doing over at the tapestry, Camille?

CAMILLE: What a beautiful portrait, Uncle. Isn't it our great-aunt?

BARON: Right. Absolutely right. She's your great-grandmother . . . or rather, your great-grandmother's sister. You see, the dear lady never . . . never contributed—except through prayer, of course—to the, er, growth of the family. My God, she was holy!

CAMILLE: Yes. A saint! My great-aunt Isabel. How lovely she looks in her habit.

BARON: Yes. . . . Perdican! What are you doing over there by the flowerpots?

PERDICAN: These are charming. Heliotrope.

BARON: Who are you kidding? Field flowers. Common as weeds.

PERDICAN: Field flowers . . . hmm. Field flowers can be very valuable, let me tell you.

BRIDAINE: Indeed. The young doctor is right. *(To Camille)* Just ask him. Ask him what sex, what class, what phylum and so on, of which elements it's composed, er . . . where the pollen comes from, the color. He'll amaze you. Almost to *confusion*, with details and phenomena of each and every sprig.

PERDICAN: No. Not so much, rev'rend sir, not so much. I know they smell good. That is all I know.

SCENE THREE

Outside the chateau.

CHORUS: A number of things amuse me, excite my curiosity. Come, sit with me, my friends, beneath the walnut tree. At this very moment two mighty trenchermen meet in the chateau: Master Bridaine and Master Blazius. You noticed that, yes? The point is: when two men so nearly identical, equally fat, equally stupid, possessed of identical vices and passions, when two such men, I say, *meet*, it follows necessarily that they will adore one another or loathe one another. Now, according to the logic by which opposites are attracted—the tall, stringy person to the little fat one, the blonde to the brunette, et cetera—so conversely, I predict a secret war between the tutor and the curé. Both are blessed with equal amounts of impudence, with barrels for stomachs, both are not only gourmets, but gourmands, so both will haggle not only over the quality of food but also the quantity. If the fish portion is small, what shall be done? You can't split a carp's tongue and one carp can't have two tongues.

Item: Both men are loudmouths, but if push comes to shove they can both talk simultaneously without listening to one another. Bridaine already tried to ask Perdican a bunch of pedantical nonsense and the tutor glowered; he doesn't want anyone else testing his pupil.

Item: They are both equally endowed with ignorance.

Item: They are both priests; one will boast about his parish, one will brag about his pupil.

Item: Master Blazius is confessor to the son; Master Bridaine to the father.

Oh, I can see them now, hunched over the table, red-cheeked and bug-eyed, their triple chins shaking with seismic hatred. They peruse one another, open with tentative sallies, proceed to formal combat, parry and thrust their pointless pedantries, while between them sits Dame Pluche completing the disaster, fending off first one, then the other, tight-lipped, with steel-tipped, lethal elbows. But now the feast is over and they're opening the gates. Here they come. Let us stand aside.

Chorus retires. Dame Pluche and the Baron enter.

BARON: Venerable Pluche, I am grieved.

PLUCHE: Impossible, my lord.

BARON: Quite possible. For so long I've looked forward to this; I even noted it in my little datebook. This day was to have been the happiest of my life. I mean it: the happiest. It was all set: my son marries my niece—good. Perfect. I talked to the curé, Master Bridaine, and now I see . . . I think I see these children cold as ice to one another. They haven't exchanged one word.

PLUCHE: See where they come. Do they know about your plan?

BARON: Oh, I dropped a word here and there . . . in private. I think it might be a good idea, since they're together now, for you and me to sit over there in the shade and leave them to it.

They retire as Camille and Perdican enter.

PERDICAN: You know, it's really not very nice; refusing to kiss me.

CAMILLE: Sorry. I'm like that. It is my . . . manner.

PERDICAN: May I offer you my arm for a little walk in the village?

CAMILLE: No. I'm tired.

PERDICAN: Wouldn't you like to see the old meadow again? Remember our picnics on the little boat? Come on, let's go down to the millpond. I'll do the rowing, and you can steer.

CAMILLE: I haven't the slightest wish to.

PERDICAN: But you're breaking my heart! Not one happy memory, one little stirring of nostalgia? Our childhood, Camille, our dear, silly little childhood—so sweet and good and so wonderfully ridiculous. . . . You don't even want to find our old path to the grange?

CAMILLE: No. Not this evening.

PERDICAN: "No. Not this evening." Well, when else? Our
whole life is out there.

CAMILLE: I'm too old to play with dolls, and too young to
live in the past.

PERDICAN: How can you say that?!

CAMILLE: I'm just telling you. Childish reminiscences
have no interest for me.

PERDICAN: They bore you?

CAMILLE: They bore me.

PERDICAN: You poor child. I'm very sorry for you.

They exit, separately.

BARON: There! You see! You hear! O excellent Dame
Pluche, I looked forward to sweet harmony. Instead
I've got a violin playing "Plaisir d'Amour" while a
flute does "Long Live the King." You know what that
sounds like? Well, it's playing right here. *(He points to
his heart)*

PLUCHE: I must tell you; I do not blame Camille. And I
thoroughly disapprove of boating parties.

BARON: What?

PLUCHE: My lord, respectable girls do not take chances
on bodies of water.

BARON: But, Pluche, bear in mind: he's going to marry
her, and so long as—

PLUCHE: It is socially improper for a young girl to take
the rudder. And unthinkable to abandon terra firma
with a man.

BARON: But I repeat—

PLUCHE: And that is my opinion.

BARON: Are you mad?! . . . You're driving me to . . . to use certain expressions which. . . . You may push me too far, Pluche! You . . . you old . . . *goose*! There. I said it. I tell you, woman, I don't know what to think of you!

They exit, separately.

SCENE FOUR

A public place. Perdican and the Chorus.

PERDICAN: Good day, my friends. Do you recognize me?

CHORUS: Sire, you look like a child we greatly loved.

PERDICAN: You! Wasn't it you who carried me piggyback over the streams? Who danced me on your knee and heaved me up behind when you went riding? You, who always made a place for me at the big table in the grange.

CHORUS: We remember, my lord. You were the worst rapscallion and finest lad in the land.

PERDICAN: Then why not embrace me, instead of bowing to me like some stranger?

CHORUS: May God bless thee, our best-loved boy! Each one here would grapple thee to his breast; but you are a man.

PERDICAN: Ten years since I've seen you, and it only takes one day for everything to change in this world. I've grown several inches towards heaven, and you a few towards the grave. Your hair is white now, your footsteps slow. You can't lift yesterday's child. It is my turn to be your father, you who once were mine.

CHORUS: This day of your return is happier than the day

of your birth; it is sweeter to greet one we know than to hold the newborn child.

PERDICAN: Look there: my lovely valleys and orchards . . . my secret pathways and the little fountain . . . all those days gone by; the secret world of a young boy's dreams . . . still full of life. My home. My *home*! Is a man really born for anything else but his one, certain corner of the world?

CHORUS: They tell us you are very learned, my lord.

PERDICAN: Yes, they tell me that, too. Oh, the sciences are wonderful, my children, but these trees and meadows teach the most important thing: to forget everything you know.

CHORUS: Some things have changed while you've been away: young girls married, young men gone to war.

PERDICAN: You can tell me all about it. I look forward to the gossip, but not quite yet. Look at that little washhouse. I used to think it was enormous. In my head there were oceans and mighty forests; now I see a little speck of water and a few blades of grass! Who's the pretty girl at the window? Over there?

CHORUS: That's Rosette. Remember? Camille's playmate when they both were little girls.

PERDICAN: Rosette! Come down, Rosette. Come here.

ROSETTE *(Entering)*: Yes, sir?

PERDICAN: You saw me from the window and wouldn't even come to say hello? Quick, let me kiss that little hand . . . and that lovely cheek.

ROSETTE *(Blushing)*: My lord . . .

PERDICAN: Are you married? They said you are.

ROSETTE: Oh no!

PERDICAN: Why not? There's no one prettier in the

whole village. We'll see to it. We'll get you married right enough.

CHORUS: My lord, she wishes to live chaste.

PERDICAN: Is that true, Rosette?

ROSETTE: Oh, no!

PERDICAN: Your sweet Camille has arrived. Have you seen her yet?

ROSETTE: She hasn't come down here yet.

PERDICAN: Go. Put on your best dress. Come sup with us at the chateau.

Perdican and Rosette exit one way; the Chorus another.

SCENE FIVE

A room in the chateau. The Baron and Master Blazius.

BLAZIUS: Sire, a word in your ear: the curé is a drunk.

BARON: Ridiculous. That's impossible.

BLAZIUS: I know it for a fact. He put down three bottles at dinner.

BARON: That is exorbitant.

BLAZIUS: And when he left the dining hall, he walked in the flowerbeds.

BARON: Walked in the flowerbeds? I am amazed. But this is very strange! Three bottles at dinner? Walking in flowerbeds? Incomprehensible. Why didn't he walk on the path?

BLAZIUS: He was weaving around too much.

BARON *(Aside)*: I'm beginning to think Bridaine was right this morning; this Blazius reeks horribly of wine.

BLAZIUS: And what's more, he stuffed himself with food. His speech was garbled.

BARON: Yes, I noticed that.

BLAZIUS: He dropped a few phrases in Latin; terrible syntax. The man's depraved.

BARON *(Aside)*: Whew! This Blazius stinks to high heaven ... *(To him)* Be advised, tutor: I have other things on my mind. I don't meddle in what people eat or what people drink. I'm not a head waiter!

BLAZIUS: Please God, I should never displease my lord the Baron. You set a good table, my lord. With good wine.

BARON: You're right. I keep a good cellar.

Bridaine enters; Blazius steps aside.

BRIDAINE: My lord, your son is in the village square, followed by every ragamuffin in town.

BARON: Impossible.

BRIDAINE: I saw him with my own eyes. They were looking for pebbles to play skipping stones.

BARON: Skipping stones! My head is swimming ... my thoughts turned upside down. . . . You bring me nonsense, Bridaine. It is unheard of for a doctor of philosophy to play at skipping stones.

BRIDAINE: Go stand at the window, sire. See for yourself.

BARON *(Aside)*: My God, Blazius was right; he *is* weaving around.

BRIDAINE: Looky there, master. Down by the washhouse. And he's got a young wench on his arm.

BARON: A young wench?! Did he come home to muck about with the farm girls? A wench on his arm and ragamuffins at his back? . . . I'm going out of my mind!

BRIDAINE: This cries out for vengeance!

BARON: All is lost! Lost without hope. . . . *I* am lost! Bridaine is weaving around; Blazius stinks to high heaven . . . and my son is seducing the farm girls with skipping stones!

Act Two

SCENE ONE

A garden: Master Blazius and Perdican.

BLAZIUS: My lord, your father's at the end of his rope.
PERDICAN: Whatever for?
BLAZIUS: You don't know he has plans to unite you with your cousin?
PERDICAN: So? Nothing could please me more.
BLAZIUS: But in the meantime he's noticed that your personalities don't seem to mesh.
PERDICAN: Too bad. I can't change mine.
BLAZIUS: So, you wish to make this union impossible?
PERDICAN: I repeat: nothing would please me more than to marry Camille. Go find my father and tell him so.
BLAZIUS: My lord, I shall withdraw. Your cousin is coming this way.

He exits as Camille enters.

PERDICAN: Already up and about, sweet coz? I still mean everything I said yesterday. You are as beautiful as love itself.

CAMILLE: Please, Perdican, let's be serious. Your father wants to marry us. I have no idea as to your thoughts on this matter, but I find it only proper to inform you: my mind's made up.

PERDICAN: And too bad for me.

CAMILLE: No worse than for any other. I do not wish to marry. There's no need for your pride to suffer.

PERDICAN: Oh damn my pride! It neither suffers nor enjoys.

CAMILLE: I came here to collect my mother's inheritance. Tomorrow I'll go back to the convent.

PERDICAN: You're a free spirit the way you come and go. Shake hands with me at least and let's be friends.

CAMILLE: I don't approve of . . . physical contact.

PERDICAN *(Taking her hand)*: Give me your hand, I say. What are you afraid of with me? You don't want them to marry us? Fine. We won't get married. Is that any reason to hate one another? Haven't we always been brother and sister? When your mother declared in her will and testament that you and I should be married, she meant she wanted us to love one another forever, and that's all she meant. Why get married? Here's your hand in mine; let us be thus united to our dying day and what need we for a priest? We need only God.

CAMILLE: I am much relieved that my refusal leaves you so . . . indifferent.

PERDICAN: Indifferent? Not at all, Camille. Your love would have been life to me, but your friendship is consolation. Don't leave tomorrow. Yesterday you refused a walk in the garden because you saw in me a husband you did not want. Stay a few days. Let me hope, at least, that our past life is not dead forever in your heart.

CAMILLE: I must leave.

PERDICAN: Why?

CAMILLE: My secret.

PERDICAN: Are you in love with someone else?

CAMILLE: No! But I must leave.

PERDICAN: Irrevocably?

CAMILLE: Irrevocably.

PERDICAN: Well then, adieu. I should have liked to spend a happy hour or two beneath the chestnut tree, talking of friendship and good times. But if that displeases you, then so be it. Goodbye, little coz.

He leaves as Pluche enters.

CAMILLE: Dame Pluche, is everything ready? Can we leave tomorrow? Has my guardian finished all the paperwork?

PLUCHE: Yes, dear little unblemished dove. Your guardian was very rude to me last evening and I am delighted to leave.

CAMILLE: Wait. Here's a note I want you to deliver. From me to Perdican. Before dinner.

PLUCHE: God in heaven! Can it be? You write notes? To a man??

CAMILLE: Am I not to be his wife? I can certainly write notes to my fiancé if I wish.

PLUCHE: But Perdican just left here. What could you possibly have to write him about? Your fiancé?! Heaven help me! Have you forgotten Jesus?

CAMILLE: Do as I say. And make all things ready. For departure.

They exit.

SCENE TWO

The dining hall. Bridaine, alone.

BRIDAINE: So! I was right! They're giving *him* the place of honor. That chair which has been mine for lo these many years, at His Lordship's right . . . and now it goes to the tutor! O God, what misery! An ass, a shameless drunkard sends me to the wrong end of the table—below the salt. His will be the first serving of wine; mine will be the cold plate, the leftovers. The cold little partridges will be quite naked; all their garnish gone. O holy Catholic church! Had this happened yesterday I could understand; he'd just arrived after so many years. O God, he's going to eat *so well*! Nothing for me but wings and backs, I just know it. I will not suffer this affront. Adieu, O venerable chair where I have so often . . . tilted back, stuffed with succulent delights. Adieu, beautiful uncorked, virginal bottles, adieu to those wonderful aromas . . . venison cooked to a turn. . . . Farewell, bountiful table, noble dining chamber. No more shall I say the Benedicite. Back to my parish house. I'll not be thrown among the rabble. I would rather, like Caesar, be first in my village, than second in Rome! *(Exit)*

SCENE THREE

A field before a cottage. Rosette and Perdican.

PERDICAN: ... Well, since your mother's not home, why not take a little walk with me?

ROSETTE: D'you think it's quite right, all these kisses you're givin' me?

PERDICAN: What harm is there in that? I'd kiss you in front of your own mother. Aren't you Camille's little playfellow, practically her sister? So that makes me like a brother to you, just as I am to her.

ROSETTE: Words is words, but kisses are kisses. I'm not what you call clever, so I look about before I speak. Now, the fine ladies who know the whole business— whether you get kissed on the right hand or the left—their fathers kiss them on the forehead, their brothers on the cheek, their lovers on the lips, and me . . . everyone kisses me on *both* cheeks and it always makes me blush.

PERDICAN: What a little beauty you are!

ROSETTE: Well, don't get worked up about that. You seem very lumpish this morning. Is the marriage off?

PERDICAN: The good folk in the village remember their love for me, even the dogs in the farmyard remember. But Camille; she does not remember. How about you? When are you getting married?

ROSETTE: Oh please! Let's not talk about that. Talk about the weather or the flowers. Or your horses. Or my new hat.

PERDICAN: Whatever you want. Anything from those lips so long as the smile remains. . . . That heavenly smile which I esteem more than life itself.

He kisses her.

ROSETTE: You may "esteem" my smile, but you sure don't "esteem" my lips. At least that's what *I* think. Only look: there's a raindrop on my hand, and the sky's as clear as day . . .

PERDICAN: I'm sorry.

ROSETTE: What have I done . . . that you weep?

They leave.

SCENE FOUR

In the chateau. Blazius and the Baron.

BLAZIUS: My lord, I have something singular to tell you. Just now I was in the pantry—I mean, in the dining hall—what would I be doing in the pantry? . . . So . . . there I was in the dining hall having found a good bottle of— . . . I mean, a good pitcher of water. . . . How could I find a bottle in the dining hall? . . . So, there I was, having a shot of red—I mean a glass of water, just to pass the time, and I looked out the window between two little flower pots, rather modern in style, but definitely influenced by the Etruscan—

BARON: What an impossible prose style you've picked up, Blazius. Completely inscrutable.

BLAZIUS: Listen to me, my lord. Give me one moment of your attention. So. There I am, looking out the window. Now don't get impatient. This concerns your family honor.

BARON: My family? My family! Absolutely incomprehensible, Blazius. My family consists of thirty-seven male branches, almost as many female, both provincial *and* from Paris.

BLAZIUS: So. Let me go on. While I was putting down a shot of wine—excuse me, a glass of water—to assist my sluggish digestion, don't you know, just imagine: I saw Dame Pluche racing by, out of breath.

BARON: Out of breath? Extraordinary.

BLAZIUS: And right beside her, flushed with anger, your niece, Camille.

BARON: Flushed with anger? My niece or Pluche?

BLAZIUS: Your niece.

BARON: My niece flushed with anger? Unheard of! How do you know it was anger? She could have been flushed for lots of reason. She's probably been chasing butterflies on the terrace.

BLAZIUS: That I can't say. Perhaps. But she was shouting: "Go on! Find him! Do as I say, you idiot! That's an order!" and she hit Pluche on the elbow with her fan, and Pluche was leaping about in the alfalfa at each command.

BARON: In the alfalfa?! And what did she reply to my niece's extravagances?

BLAZIUS: She said: "I don't want to. I'll never find him. He's paying court to every girl in the village . . . even the one who raises turkeys. I'm too old to be a go-between. My hands are clean!" And as she shouted, she was clutching a piece of paper, *folded in half.*

BARON: I don't understand this. Why should Dame Pluche fold papers in half and leap about in the alfalfa? I cannot give credence to such monstrosities.

BLAZIUS: Don't you see? It's clear as day, my lord, what this means.

BARON: In truth, my friend, I don't understand one damn thing. It seems crazy. No rhyme nor reason.

BLAZIUS: What it means is: your niece is having a *liaison*.

BARON: What?! Do you know what you're saying? Weigh your words with care, priest.

BLAZIUS: I weigh them in that same celestial balance where my soul shall one day be judged. And I find nothing but plain fact: your niece is having a liaison.

BARON: Oh, but please do realize, my friend . . . that is impossible!

BLAZIUS: Then why did she give the governess a letter? Why did she shout "Find him" and why did the old lady scowl?

BARON: But to whom was this letter addressed?

BLAZIUS: Aye, there's the rub. "*Hic jacet lepus,*" ["Here lies the hare," i.e. "Here's what we're looking for!"] as they say. To whom was the letter addressed? To some man who pays court to turkey keepers. Now, I say a man who lusts after turkey keepers is probably destined to keep turkeys himself. Moreover, it is inconceivable that a girl with your niece's education should be going after such a man. That is what I say, and why I say, saving your reverence, that I don't understand anything any better than you do.

BARON: Heavens! Just this morning my niece told me she refuses to marry Perdican. Why? So she can keep turkeys? Let us go to my chambers. I've been through so many upheavals since yesterday, I don't know up from down!

SCENE FIVE

A fountain in the woods. Perdican, alone, reading a note.

PERDICAN: "Be at the little fountain at noon." Now what does *this* mean? A cold shoulder, a cruel and definite refusal, overweening pride, and then, to top it off, a rendezvous! If it's just casual, why this place? And if it's flirtation . . . well. This morning, walking with Rosette, I thought I heard something behind us rustling in the bushes, but I thought it was the little doe. . . . Is something "afoot"? . . . I certainly hope so!

Camille enters.

CAMILLE: Hello, coz. It seemed to me, whether rightly or wrongly, that you left me rather sadly this morning. You took my hand—which I never proffered—and now I have come to take yours. And I refused you a kiss. Here. *(She has taken his hand, and now kisses his cheek)* Finally, you said you wished to talk of our friendship. Good. Sit here, and let's talk.

PERDICAN: Is this a dream? Are you really talking to me?

CAMILLE: You find it . . . singular, no doubt, to receive a note from me? Well, perhaps my moods are fickle, but you said something this morning that's absolutely correct. "Let us part as friends" you said, but you still don't know why we must part. Now I'll tell you. I have decided to take the veil.

PERDICAN: You?! My little Camille? Sitting there by our fountain . . . sitting surrounded by flowers as in all those summers gone by?

CAMILLE: Yes, Perdican, it's me, come to relive a quarter

hour or so of "all those summers gone by." I know I must have appeared haughty and brusque to you, but you've got to understand. I have renounced the world. Still, before leaving it forever, I should be pleased to hear your opinion. Do you think I've made the right choice? Will I make a good nun?

PERDICAN: Don't ask me; I'd make a terrible monk!

CAMILLE: We've scarcely seen one another for ten years and you have begun to . . . taste life. I know what sort of man you are and how quickly you must have learned about the world with such a heart, such a vigorous spirit as is yours. Tell me, have you had any mistresses?

PERDICAN: I beg your pardon?

CAMILLE: Answer me truthfully, without modesty or pretension.

PERDICAN: Well . . . I've had a few, yes.

CAMILLE: Were you in love with them?

PERDICAN: Madly.

CAMILLE: Where are they now? Do you know?

PERDICAN: Really, what an extraordinary question: "Where are they now?" How on earth should I know? I was neither husband nor brother to any of them. They are . . . wherever they damn well please.

CAMILLE: There must have been one you loved more than the others. How long did you love the one you loved more than the others?

PERDICAN: You are the strangest girl! What are you, my confessor?

CAMILLE: It's a favor I'm asking; answer me truthfully. You're not a libertine, and I know you have an honest heart. You have inspired love in others, of course you have, and you deserve it. And you would never just indulge yourself. So, answer me.

PERDICAN: Honestly, I just don't remember.

CAMILLE: Have you ever known anyone . . . any man . . . who loved only one woman?

PERDICAN: Oh, I'm sure there must be . . . some.

CAMILLE: Some friend of yours, perhaps. What's his name?

PERDICAN: Look, I can't give you any names, but I'm sure there are some men capable of falling in love only once.

CAMILLE: How many times can a virtuous man fall in love?

PERDICAN: What do you want from me, rules? Catalogues? Is this some sort of catechism lesson?

CAMILLE: I want to be instructed. I want to know if I'm right or wrong to follow my vocation. If I were to marry you wouldn't you have to answer all my questions candidly? Wouldn't you lay open your heart to me? I respect you, Perdican, and I believe, with your education and from your very nature, that you stand head and shoulders above most other men. It upsets me you can't remember the things I'm asking, but perhaps if we keep on talking I'll begin to understand.

PERDICAN: Just tell me what you're driving at and I'll gladly answer

CAMILLE: So. Let's go back to the first question. Have I made the right choice? Should I stay in the convent?

PERDICAN: No.

CAMILLE: I'd be better off marrying you?

PERDICAN: Yes.

CAMILLE: If the curé of your parish were to lay his hands over a glass of water and tell you it was now a glass of wine, would you believe him and drink up?

PERDICAN: No.

CAMILLE: If the curé of your parish were to lay his hands upon you and tell me that you'd love me your whole life long, should I believe him?

PERDICAN: Yes and no.

CAMILLE: And what would you advise me to do on the day I find out you're no longer in love with me.

PERDICAN: I would advise you to take a lover.

CAMILLE: And the day I find out my lover's no longer in love with me?

PERDICAN: Take another.

CAMILLE: And this process, how long should it go on?

PERDICAN: Till your hair has turned to gray, and mine to white.

CAMILLE: Do you know what the cloister is like? Have you ever spent any time there, in a convent chapel?

PERDICAN: Of course. I've been to one.

CAMILLE: I have a friend there, a young sister, not yet thirty. She inherited five hundred thousand crowns on her fifteenth birthday. She is the noblest, most beautiful creature who ever walked this earth. She's a member of the peerage and her husband was one of the most distinguished men in France. No skill or talent was left undeveloped in her, like some special breed of plant where every shoot turns to leaf and then to flower. Never did happiness and love crown a fairer brow. Her husband deceived her; she went to another man for love. She is dying of despair.

PERDICAN: Quite possibly.

CAMILLE: We share the same cell, and have lain awake nights talking of her grief which has become almost my own. Isn't that odd? I'm not sure how it happened exactly. When she told me about her wedding, described the delirious joy of those first days, the peace and comfort which followed, and then how it all simply vanished . . . how one evening she was sitting by the fire, and he by the window, and not one word passed between them . . . not one word . . . how their love began to fade and how each attempt to rekindle it turned into anger, ugly scenes; how a stranger came between them, insinuated herself into their pain . . . well, when she told me all these things, I saw *me*. It was me there. When she said: "Oh how happy I was then!," *my* heart leapt for joy. And when she said, "I wept at that," the tears which fell were mine. And listen to this, something even stranger: I began to create an imaginary existence. This went on for four years. I won't bore you with all the fantasies, the remarkable fact: whenever Louise told me her story, or whenever I dreamed my own dream . . . the face I saw was yours.

PERDICAN: Mine?

CAMILLE: Oh, it's perfectly natural of course. What other man have I known? But it is true, Perdican. I did love you.

PERDICAN: How old are you, Camille?

CAMILLE: Eighteen.

PERDICAN: Go on. I'm listening.

CAMILLE: There are two hundred women in our convent. A small portion of them have never . . . known the world, but all of them wait only for death. More than one of them has left the cloister, as I have even now, young virgins, filled with expectation. They come back in a very short time, already aging, already disillusioned. Every day there is a death in our community and every day a novice arrives to assume the little horsehair mattress that's been left. Visitors who come admire the calm and the order of our house. They admire the whiteness of our veils, but wonder why we wear them always lowered. What do you think of these women, Perdican? Are they correct? Or misguided?

PERDICAN: I know nothing about it.

CAMILLE: Some there are who tell me to live chaste. But I want your opinion. Do you think such women would have been better off just taking a lover? And should they counsel me to do likewise?

PERDICAN: I know *nothing about it.*

CAMILLE: You promised you would answer.

PERDICAN: Yes, but I have a natural excuse: I simply don't believe this is you speaking.

CAMILLE: That is possible. And surely there must be, amongst all my thoughts and notions, some which are merely ridiculous. It's also possible that I've been taught a lesson by rote and parrot it mistakenly. *(Pause)* In our main hall there is a painting which shows a monk hunched over his missal, but through the bars of his window you can just make out a little patch of sunlight, and there, in the distance, a sort of rustic inn and in front of that, a goat-boy dancing. Which do you prefer: the monk or the goatherd?

PERDICAN: Neither. And both. They are two creatures of flesh and blood; one who studies and one who dances. That's all there is to that. And I think you're quite right to become a nun.

CAMILLE: Just a moment ago you said I was quite wrong.

PERDICAN: Did I? Well, perhaps I did.

CAMILLE: So that's what you advise?

PERDICAN: So you have *nothing* to believe?

CAMILLE: Look at me, Perdican. What person on earth believes in nothing?

PERDICAN: This one. I don't believe in "life everlasting" at any rate. My dear little cousin, the sisters have taught you by their experience but believe me, it doesn't have to be *yours*. You'll never make it through life without falling in love.

CAMILLE: Oh, I want to be in love, but I don't want to suffer for it. I want a love that's eternal and vows that don't get broken. Here is my lover. *(She shows him her crucifix)*

PERDICAN: That lover . . . does not preclude others.

CAMILLE: For me He does. For me He shall. Don't smile at me, Perdican. For ten years we've been apart and tomorrow I leave once more. Perhaps, in another ten years, we shall speak of this again. I did not want you to remember me as some statue, cold and insensitive. It is insensitivity which has led me to this point in my life. Listen to me: go back to your world and, insomuch as you can, be happy. And, insomuch as you can, love. And in so doing, forget your dearest Camille. But if ever you abandon love, or find yourself abandoned, if ever the angel of hope forsakes you utterly and there is emptiness in your heart, think on me. I shall be praying for you.

PERDICAN: You're extremely vain; watch out for that.

CAMILLE: Why do you say that?

PERDICAN: You are eighteen years old, and you don't believe in love.

CAMILLE: And you do? You tell me that you do? Resting there comfortably on those knees that are nearly worn out with bowing and scraping before a hundred

mistresses whose names you can't even remember! O
and you've wept deep tears of despair, but you always
knew the well would never run dry. You play the
young man-about-town and smile at tales of a
maiden's tears. You can't believe in "dying for love"
because you've loved and Look: you're still alive! O
Lord, the ways of this world! I should think you'd
rather scorn those women who take you as you are,
who shoo away their former lovers and take you in
their arms with breaths still hot from someone else's
kisses. I asked you whether you had ever loved. You
answered like a tourist, as if I had inquired after Italy
or Peru: "Oh yes, I've been there, and next year
Germany, and after that who knows?" What is love to
you? Some kind of currency passed from hand to
hand till death do you part? No. Not even that. For
even the smallest coin, passed from hand to hand,
retains its proper portrait.

PERDICAN: How beautiful you are, how alive!

CAMILLE: Yes, I'm beautiful, don't I know it. Flatterers
tell me nothing. The silent nun who cuts our hair will
pale no doubt when she sees these lovely tresses. But
they shall not be exchanged for rings and jewels and
commerce of the boudoir. Not one lock shall remain
after the razor's triumph. And when the priest shall
place my celestial bridegroom's ring upon my finger,
let him take my tresses for his priestly robes.

PERDICAN: Look at you . . . you're on fire!

CAMILLE: I was wrong to talk to you; I've told you
everything, my whole life with these words. O
Perdican, don't laugh at me. It is as sad as death.

PERDICAN: My poor child. I've let you speak and now I
must reply. You tell me of some nun who had, or so I

think, a deadly influence. You say she was deceived, herself a deceiver in turn, and then she fell to despair. Are you so absolutely sure that if her husband or her lover reappeared, and reached with his hand through the cloister grille, are you so absolutely sure she would not seize it?

CAMILLE: What are you saying? I did not hear that!

PERDICAN: Are you so absolutely sure that if her husband, or her lover, invited her to suffer one more time, she would refuse?

CAMILLE: Of course!

PERDICAN: There are two hundred women in your convent, most of whom were wounded to the heart. They have made you touch those wounds and have smeared your virgin thoughts with their heart's blood. Oh, and they have *lived*, and shown you the horrors of their passage. You cross yourself before their wounds as if they were the holy wounds of Jesus. They've dragged you along their dreary Stations of the Cross and when you see a living man, you faint with religious fear, clutching at your haggard sisters' skirts. Are you sure that if the man they curse, the man whose deceit they mourn and whose soul they damn on bended knee, are you sure that if they were to see him one more time they would not break their chains asunder to run at those lost pains, and press their bleeding hearts against his dagger? O my child, do you know the dreams of women who tell you not to dream? Do you know what names they murmur when their trembling tongues falter at the sacramental Host? These palsied hags who pour their blasted youth into your ear, who sound the knell of their despair in the ruins of your youth and who startle the

warmth of your blood with the chill of their graves,
do you know what these nuns are?

CAMILLE: You frighten me. . . . You too, you are on
fire . . .

PERDICAN: Do you know what these nuns are, you
wretched girl! These nuns who tell you that man's
love is man's deceit, do they know that there is a
deceit far greater still, the deceit of divine love? Do
they know it is a sin to whisper in a maiden's ear the
secrets of a woman? Oh, what lessons they've taught
you! And I knew it the moment I saw you stand
transfixed before that portrait, our venerable
great-aunt. You wanted to leave without so much as
taking my hand, didn't want even to see our woods,
our little fountain here which weeps for *us*. You
renounce our childhood and that death mask which
the nuns have cast upon your cheeks would not allow
so much as a brotherly kiss. But your heart would not
be stilled. Your heart, which never learned to read,
forgot those lessons and led you here to sit upon the
grass, and here we are. So then. These women have
spoken. They have set you on the straight and
narrow. It has cost me my life's happiness. But tell
them this from me: heaven is not for them.

CAMILLE: Nor for me, neither?

PERDICAN: Adieu, Camille. Go to your cloister. And
when they speak their poison to you, answer them
with this: all men are false, inconstant, lying
hypocrites, vain or shameless, despicable and
lecherous; all women are faithless, artificial,
conceited, meddling and depraved. The world is a
fathomless, running sewer, where cunning sea lions
romp and disport themselves on occasional islands of

filth. But there is in this world one thing that is holy and sublime: it is the *union* of two of these beings, imperfect and despicable though they may be. One is often cheated by love, often wounded, often grieved. *But one loves.* And then, on the threshold of death, one can look back and say: I have sinned and I have strayed, but I have loved. It was *me* there. Not some figment of my pride or my ennui. It was *me*!

He leaves her there.

Act Three

SCENE ONE

Before the chateau; the Baron and Master Blazius.

BARON: Over and above your drunkenness, Master Blazius, you are an out-and-out cad. My servants saw you creep into the larder and you now stand convicted of attempting to steal—in a manner which can only be described as pathetic—several bottles of my wine. And then, having been thus convicted, you try to justify your presence there by attributing to my niece some sort of secret correspondence.

BLAZIUS: But, my lord, I beg you to remember—

BARON: Leave, despicable abbot. And do not come into my sight again. It is mad to behave as you have behaved, and the dignity of my position forbids all pardon.

He leaves, Blazius following, protesting. Perdican enters.

PERDICAN: I should very much like to know if I'm in

love. On the plus side, there's the way she interrogated me, rather brazen for a girl of eighteen. On the minus side there are all those weird ideas the nuns have crammed into her head. Hard to correct all that twaddle. Worst of all, she leaves today! Damn! Oh, of course I love her. I'm sure I love her. After all, who knows? Maybe she was just reciting some lesson or other. Still it's absolutely clear she doesn't give a damn about me. Besides, even her good looks can't changer her bad manners and that willful way she's got. I've just got to stop thinking about her. . . . Of course I don't love her. She *is* pretty, though. And why can't I get that conversation out of my head? I spoke nothing but drivel all last night. . . . What am I doing? . . . Where am I going? . . . Ah! To the village. *(He exits)*

SCENE TWO

Bridaine, alone, on a pathway.

BRIDAINE: Alas! Noon! Now what are they doing? They'll all be at table. I wonder what they're eating. I wonder what they're not eating. I saw the cook come by with a huge turkey. His helper had a basket of truffles . . . and raisins.

Blazius enters on the other side of the stage. The two are unaware of each other's presence.

BLAZIUS: O unforeseen disgrace! Exiled from the chateau! Which means, of course, exiled from the dining hall! No more wine from the larder.

BRIDAINE: No more the sweet aroma of those dishes. No more the warmth of the great fireplace upon my sated tummy.

BLAZIUS: Why did fatal curiosity make me overhear Dame Pluche and the little niece? Why did I report it all to the Baron?!

BRIDAINE: Why did vain conceit persuade me to leave that welcoming table? Who cares if I sit on the right or the left?!

BLAZIUS: Alas, I *was* a bit tight when I committed such folly.

BRIDAINE: Alas, I *was* a bit snockered when I acted so imprudently.

BLAZIUS *(Seeing Bridaine)*: My God, it's the curé!

BRIDAINE *(Seeing Blazius)*: My Lord, it's the tutor!

BLAZIUS: Ah, monsieur the curé, what are you doing here?

BRIDAINE: Me? Oh, going to dinner, going to dinner. Aren't you coming?

BLAZIUS: No. Not today. Alas, Master Bridaine, do intercede for me. The Baron kicked me out! I falsely accused Mademoiselle Camille of carrying on a secret correspondence, but God is my witness I did see, or thought I saw, Dame Pluche in the alfalfa. I am lost, monsieur the curé, lost!

BRIDAINE: What are you telling me?

BLAZIUS: The truth! The truth, alas, the truth! I am in utter disgrace for having pilfered a bottle of wine.

BRIDAINE: What is all this? Bottles of wine . . . secret correspondence . . . alfalfa?

BLAZIUS: I beg you, I implore you: plead my case. I'm really an honest man. O worthy Master Bridaine, I am your servant forever!

BRIDAINE *(Aside)*: Oh joy! Is this a dream? O happy chair
    at table, I shall once more sit on thee!

BLAZIUS: I shall be beholden to you; listen to my story. I
    know you'll see fit to absolve me, dear my lord. Holy
    father!

BRIDAINE: Impossible, monsieur. The bell has struck
    noon and I must go to dinner. If the Baron has some
    complaint against you, that is your affair. I do not
    intercede for drunks! *(Aside)* Quickly now, to the grill,
    and thou, my stomach, grow and prosper! *(He runs off)*

BLAZIUS: O wretched Pluche! You're going to pay for
    this. You are the cause of my downfall, shameless
    hussy! Vile panderer, to you do I owe my disgrace. O
    holy University of Paris! Me . . . a drunkard? Unless I
    can come up with a letter and prove to the Baron that
    his niece has been up to something, I'm done for. I
    saw her in the little room this morning writing
    something. Aha! Patience now, here's something . . .

Dame Pluche walks by carrying a letter.

Pluche! Give me that letter!

PLUCHE: What does this mean? This is my young
    mistress' letter and I am going to post it.

BLAZIUS: The letter or your life!

PLUCHE: My life?! My life!! O Jesus and Mary, virgin and
    martyr!

BLAZIUS: Yes, Pluche, your life. Now give me that letter.

They struggle over the letter. Perdican enters.

PERDICAN: What's going on? What on earth are you

doing, Master Blazius? Why are you violating this
woman?

PLUCHE: Give me back that letter! He stole it from me.
Justice, I cry; justice!

BLAZIUS: She's a go-between, my lord. This is no letter;
this is a billet-doux.

PLUCHE: It's a *letter* from Camille, my lord. From your
fiancée.

BLAZIUS: It's a billet-doux to a turkey farmer!

PLUCHE: You lie, abbot. Mark my word.

PERDICAN: Give me the letter. I don't know why you're
fighting, but as Camille's fiancé I reserve the right to
read the address: "To Sister Louise at the Convent of
Saint-Mandé." *(Aside)* Damn my curiosity! What's this
going to prove? My heart is pounding . . . steady . . .
steady. *(To the others)* Pray you, retire, Dame Pluche.
You are an honorable woman and Master Blazius is a
ninny. Go in and dine. I'll see this letter's posted.

Pluche and Blazius exit, separately.

That it's criminal to open someone else's letter I know
as well as I know my own name. What would Camille
have to say to her Sister Louise? Oh God, I must be in
love! What strange force has wrapped this girl around
me so that just reading an address my fingers start to
tremble? Now this is interesting: in his tussle with
Dame Pluche old Blazius knocked the seal off. It's no
crime to just . . . unfold. No one will ever notice.

    (He opens it and reads) "I leave today my dearest, and
everything has happened just as I predicted. It's a
terrible state of affairs; the young man is wounded to

the heart. He'll never get over losing me, even though I did everything in my power to make him loathe me. God will pardon me for having driven him to despair. Alas, my dearest, what else could I do? Pray for me. We'll be together again tomorrow, and this time for always! To you my fondest thoughts, soul of my soul, Camille."

How dare she! How dare she write about me like that! "Driven to despair" . . . me? If that were true she'd know it. She did everything in her power to make me loathe her? I'm "wounded to the heart"? Why on earth would she invent such romantic nonsense? O women, women! What a perfect saint is this little Camille: she gives herself to God in good faith, but she wants to make good and sure that I'm left miserable. I'm sure she and her convent friends thought this up before she left. Oh yes, they planned it all: Camille goes to see her cousin; he wants to marry her; she refuses and cousin is left in despair. Very interesting that; a young girl sacrifices her own cousin to Almighty God. Oh no, Camille, I do *not* love you. I am *not* in despair. My heart is *not* wounded and what's more: I'll prove it to you! *(He tears off a part of the paper and writes on it)* You'll see before you even leave here that, in fact, I'm in love with someone else. Hey there, you! Good fellow!

A peasant enters.

Go to the chateau. Tell them in the kitchen to send a servant with this note to Mademoiselle Camille.

PEASANT: Yes sir. *(Exit)*

PERDICAN: And now to the next one. "I'm driven to

despair." Ha! *(He goes to a little doorway and knocks)*
Rosette? . . . Rosette!?

ROSETTE *(Opening door)*: Is that you then, my lord. . . .
Come in. My mother's here.

PERDICAN: Put on your prettiest bonnet, Rosette, and
come with me.

ROSETTE: But . . . where?

PERDICAN: I'll tell you later. Ask your mum for
permission, there's a good girl. But hurry!

ROSETTE: Yes, m'lord. *(She goes into the house)*

PERDICAN: I've asked Camille to meet me one more time
by the little fountain, and I'm sure she'll come. But,
by heaven, she won't find what she expects. I shall
woo Rosette before her very eyes.

*Rosette comes out of the cottage, a bright new bonnet on her
head.*

Beautiful! *(He kisses her)* Perfect!!

They run off.

SCENE THREE

*In the woods. By the fountain. Camille strolls on; from the other side,
the peasant.*

PEASANT: Hey, mam'selle! I'm goin' to the chateau with a
letter fer you. What d'ya think? Shall I give it to you,
or take it to the kitchen? What d'ya think? What'll I
do?

CAMILLE: Give it to me.

PEASANT: Now, if you'd rather, I'll just skedaddle on up there instead of stoppin' here. What d'ya think?

CAMILLE: I said to give it to me.

PEASANT: Oh well, whatever you want.

CAMILLE *(Gives him a coin)*: Here's for your trouble.

PEASANT: Oh, yeah, well, thank'ee. I'll go now. What d'ya think?

CAMILLE: As you wish!

PEASANT: Well, then . . . guess I'll go. Yeah, guess I'll go. *(He goes)*

CAMILLE *(Reading)*: . . . He wants me to meet him at the fountain where we met yesterday. What does he want to tell me? Oh well, I'm right here anyway. I wonder, though, should I really consent to—. Ah! There he comes now . . . with Rosette. I suppose he'll send her away . . . *(She hides behind a tree)* I certainly don't want it to look like I got here first!

Perdican and Rosette enter, and sit by the fountain.

Well, what's this all about? Sitting next to her? Did he ask me here to talk with someone else?

PERDICAN: I love you, Rosette. You're the only one who still remembers how happy we all were, all those happy days we'll never see again. So now I want you to share a new life with me. Love me, sweet child. Here. Here is a pledge of my love. *(He puts his golden chain around her neck)*

ROSETTE: Your golden chain . . . for me?

PERDICAN: And you see this ring? Look into the water here. See our reflections, so close to one another, our faces, our hands touching. . . . Now look! *(He throws the ring into the water)* The picture's shattered. But look: little by little it's coming back into focus. The water ... settles. Just a little trembling still, the circles flowing out to the edge ... patience ... patience, we'll soon reappear like magic. Already I see our arms intertwined and in just a second there won't be a single wrinkle left on your beautiful, sweet face. ... There! *(He turns front)* That ring was given to me by Camille.

CAMILLE *(Aside)*: My ring ... he threw it away!

PERDICAN: Do you know what love is, Rosette? Listen: the air is still. The gentle morning rain has stopped and water-drops fall like tiny pearls from the leaves as the sun revives them. By that heavenly light, by that sun I swear I love thee. You are, I think, fond of me at least? *(He speaks somewhat more loudly)* No one has blasted the flower of your youth, or poisoned the vigor of your young heart's blood. Not you for a nunnery, never! But fresh, and radiant for a young man's arms. O Rosette, Rosette, do you know what love is?

ROSETTE: Alas, young doctor, sir ... I'll love you ... good as I can.

PERDICAN: "Good as you can"? ... Nay, better! Doctor of law though I be, and child of the land though you be, you will love me better far than ... than these *pale little statuettes fabricated by nuns* ... with *heads* where their *hearts should be*! Who emerge from their dark little cells to permeate the air. You know nothing; you read nothing but the prayer book your mother taught you, which her mother taught her. You don't understand the words you say when you kneel at your bed in prayer, but you know that you pray and that is what pleases God.

ROSETTE: You're talking so wild, my lord . . .

PERDICAN: Books you don't know, but these woods and
grasses, quiet streams and generous fields at harvest
time, these you know and this is the proper
knowledge of youth. This world is your family, and
me, now, a part of it. Rise up, now, for you will be my
wife, and we shall strike roots to tap the wonders of
this world, and grow, and prosper!

He leads her off. Camille retrieves the ring, and exits.

SCENE FOUR

The Chorus enters.

CHORUS: Surely something strange transpires. Camille
has refused the hand of Perdican; she must run to
her convent from whence she so shortly sprung. But I
hear that the young man consoles himself with
Rosette. Poor waif, she knows not what snares await
her, heeding a young gallant's apostrophe.

Dame Pluche comes bustling on.

PLUCHE: Quick! Quick! Saddle my ass!

CHORUS: Do you pass among us like a zephyr in spring,
O venerable Pluche? And must you bestride your
pitiable ass betimes, who weeps at the thought of
your progress?

PLUCHE: I thank my Maker, you scum, that I may leave
and was not meant to die in this place.

CHORUS: Die far away, Pluche, my lovely, my sweet. Die

all alone in some unwholesome cave, unshriven and unmourned. We shall pray for your dignified resurrection.

Camille is seen.

PLUCHE: Ah, my mistress is here. Dearest Camille, all is prepared for leavetaking. The Baron has closed his accounts and my ass has been properly saddled.

CAMILLE: You and your ass can go to hell; I'm not going anywhere today! *(She exits)*

CHORUS: What does this signify? Dame Pluche is waxen with terror. Her false hairs attempt to stand. Her bosom heaves and there is a mighty wringing of hands.

PLUCHE: Lord Jesus! Camille *swore*!! *(She runs off)*

SCENE FIVE

The Baron and Bridaine.

BRIDAINE: My lord, I must speak to you in private. Your son is paying court to a girl from the village.

BARON: Ridiculous.

BRIDAINE: I saw him, clear as day, walking through the heather. And he offered her his arm.

BARON: Monstrous.

BRIDAINE: Here's the clincher: he gave her a rather generous gift which she took home and showed to her mother.

BARON: Good God! "Rather generous"? How generous?

BRIDAINE: Both in value and in meaning: the golden chain he always wears.

BARON: Let's go into my study. I don't know what to believe anymore.

They exit.

SCENE SIX

Camille's chamber; Camille and Dame Pluche.

CAMILLE: You say he took my letter?

PLUCHE: Yes, my child. He said he'd see it posted.

CAMILLE: Go into the sitting room, Dame Pluche, and be so good as to tell Perdican I wish to see him here.

Pluche exits.

He read the letter, that's for sure. That little scene in the woods was his revenge. So is his "love" for Rosette. He wants to prove he can love someone else, that he's indifferent to me in spite of everything. Hmm. Maybe he *is* in love with me after all. *(She goes to a small, curtained-off recess)* Are you there, Rosette?

ROSETTE *(Revealed)*: Yes. Can I come in?

CAMILLE: Listen, my girl. Perdican's courting you, isn't he?

ROSETTE: Alas, yes.

CAMILLE: What do you think of all those things he said to you this morning?

ROSETTE: This morning? Where this morning?

CAMILLE: Don't play games, Rosette. This morning by the little fountain.

ROSETTE: You saw me?

CAMILLE: How naive you are, poor thing. No, I didn't see you. I just know. He recited a lot of fancy speeches, didn't he? I'll bet he even promised to marry you.

ROSETTE: How did you know?!

CAMILLE: Never mind how I know. Do you believe him?

ROSETTE: Why shouldn't I believe him? Is he going to deceive me? Why would he do that?

CAMILLE: Perdican will never marry you, my dear.

ROSETTE: Oh God, I don't understand anything.

CAMILLE: You're in love with him, poor thing, and he'll never marry you. The proof? Here. I'll show you. Hide behind the little curtain there. Just give a listen, and when I call for you, come forth.

Rosette hides.

Perhaps this isn't vengeance at all, but an act of kindness. Poor thing, she's fallen for him.

Perdican enters.

Good day, coz. Sit down, please.

PERDICAN: Well, look at you! Dressed fit to kill. Whom, I wonder.

CAMILLE: You perhaps. I'm so sorry I missed our little rendezvous this morning. You had something you wished to say?

Perdican smiles knowingly.

PERDICAN: Oh no, no. Nothing really. Except: "Farewell,

Camille." I thought you were leaving. But now I see your horses are still in the stable and those certainly aren't traveling clothes.

CAMILLE: No matter. I love a good conversation and I'm not sure but I wouldn't really like to argue with you one more time.

PERDICAN: What's the fun of arguing when there's no possibility of making up? The whole fun of a fight is . . . what comes after.

CAMILLE: And are you so sure I wouldn't like that too?

PERDICAN: Do not mock me, lady. I'm not good at repartee.

CAMILLE: Oh. I was hoping to be courted. I don't know, maybe it's this new gown, but I feel like having fun! Yesterday you asked me to go down to the village. Good. Let's go. Let's take out the boat and find a good picnic spot, take a walk in the woods, anything. Will there be a moon this evening, do you think? Oh! Now that's odd. You're not wearing the ring I gave you.

PERDICAN: I lost it.

CAMILLE: Yes. And that's why I found it. Here. Here it is. *(She presents it to him)*

PERDICAN: Really? . . . You found it?

CAMILLE: You're looking to see if my hands are wet, aren't you. The truth is, you see, I ruined the dress I had on pulling this little plaything from the fountain. That's why I had to change . . . yes, that's a good choice of words: I've changed. Go on. Put it on your finger.

PERDICAN: You fished this ring out from the. . . . But you could have fallen in. Is this a dream? Is it really you giving me this ring once more? Why? Why keep some token of a time that's gone forever? Answer me. What is all this, all these games: "I'm leaving," "I'm staying," like some little coquette.

CAMILLE: What do you know of women, Perdican? Are you so sure we are inconstant? Do you know if we really change our minds and our words as often as you think? There are some who would tell you, no. Oh yes, we have to play the part, even fib sometimes. You see I'm being frank with you. But are you sure that when our tongues lie, our hearts lie as well? Have you ever thought, really thought about these temperamental and violent beings you imagine, about how harshly we are judged, how tightly regulated? And maybe, just maybe—brainless little things that we are—when driven to distraction by the world, we lie just for the fun of it. Just for relief, as sometimes we must lie for necessity.

PERDICAN: I won't even listen to all that. I never lie. And I love you, Camille. That is the only real thing I know.

CAMILLE: You say you love me. And you never lie?

PERDICAN: Never.

CAMILLE: Yet here's someone who says you often do.

She opens the curtain, revealing Rosette, who stands there in shock, unable to speak.

What have you to say to this child, Perdican? If you never lie, why is she struck dumb, hearing you pledge your love to me? I'll leave the two of you alone. Answer for yourself. *(She starts to leave)*

PERDICAN: No. Wait! Listen to me!

CAMILLE: What can you possibly have to say? It is to her you must speak.

Rosette bolts out of the room in tears.

I do not care for you, sir. I didn't drag that wretched girl from her cottage and use her like some puppet, some doll. I didn't speak hot words to her intended for someone else's ear; I didn't pretend to cast away a long-respected love; I didn't put a golden chain around her neck and I did not ask her to marry me!

PERDICAN: Listen to me; please listen!

CAMILLE: I saw that little smirk when I told you I was unable to meet you at the fountain. Yes, of course I was there, and heard every word, but I would not for the life of me have spoken as you spoke to that poor girl. What will you say to her now when you find her, your kisses fresh upon her lips, and now these woundings to her heart? You wanted to spite me, to punish me for a letter written to my convent. You wanted to wound me any way possible and you didn't give a damn if your arrow had first to pass through that poor innocent, just so long as it finally hit the mark. I flattered myself to think I had inspired in you some bit of love, and of regret. That, your pride could not suffer! Well. Hear this from me now: yes, you do love me and yes, you will marry that poor girl or else you are beneath contempt.

PERDICAN: Yes! Yes, I shall marry her.

CAMILLE: And well you should.

PERDICAN: Well I should? Nay, better. Much better than ever marrying you. What's wrong, Camille? Why this sudden ardor, why so hot? The child was shocked, she ran away . . . that happens. You wanted to prove to her that, once in my life, I told a lie. Very good. Perhaps once I did. But you're a bit presumptuous to

think you know . . . *which* time. And now if you'll
excuse me . . .

The Baron enters, unseen by Perdican.

. . . I must attend to my fiancée.

Perdican leaves. Camille turns to the Baron.

BARON: If that's true . . . I shall go stark, staring mad . . .
CAMILLE: Use your authority.
BARON: Mad, that's it. I'll go mad. But, I won't give my
consent.
CAMILLE: You must speak to him and bring him to his
senses.
BARON: This will ruin everything. The whole Harvest
Festival is ruined! I don't dare show my face at court.
Such a marriage is . . . is disproportionate. Who ever
heard of marrying your cousin's playmate. It breaks
every social regulation.
CAMILLE: Send for him and tell him straight out you're
displeased with this union. Believe me it's just a
madness, but he doesn't know how to resist.
BARON: I'll wear black all winter, that's what I'll do.
CAMILLE: For God's sake, speak to him!! It's just a folly
with him, but it may already be too late! He says he'll
go through with it and he probably will.
BARON: I am going to my room and lose myself in grief.
Tell him, should he ask, that I've had a collapse, that
I am wracked with sorrow to see him marry a girl of
no position. Wracked by sorrow. Wracked! *(He exits)*
CAMILLE: Oh where can I find a *man* around here?!
When you need one, the solitude is terrifying.

Perdican enters.

Well, cousin . . . when's the wedding?

PERDICAN: Soon as possible. I've already notified the notary, the priest and the entire village.

CAMILLE: You really mean to go through with this?

PERDICAN: Absolutely.

CAMILLE: What will your father say?

PERDICAN: Whatever he likes. Marrying Rosette appeals to me. I owe the whole idea to you and nothing will change my mind. I won't bore you with all the clichés about her station in life and mine. She's young, she's pretty and she loves me, which are three things more than most husbands get. Whether or not she's terribly bright, who cares? I could've done a lot worse. People will cry and people will laugh; I wash my hands.

CAMILLE: There's no reason for people to laugh. You're absolutely right to marry her. But I do worry about one thing. I worry that you're doing this out of spite.

PERDICAN: Worry about it all you like; it means nothing to me.

CAMILLE: But you're not thinking this through; the girl's a nobody.

PERDICAN: She'll become a somebody when she marries me.

CAMILLE: You'll be bored with her before the notary even gets here! You'll feel your gorge rising at the wedding feast, and afterwards you'll want to get rid of her because she smells of the kitchen.

PERDICAN: You'll see how wrong you are. You don't know me at all. If a woman is sweet and caring, fresh and pretty and good, that's all I need, and I couldn't care less whether or not she knows Latin.

CAMILLE: Pity so much money has been spent teaching it to you. Three thousand crowns for nothing.

PERDICAN: Quite right. Much better to have given it to the poor.

CAMILLE: Meaning *you*: the poor in spirit.

PERDICAN: Then I shall inherit the earth.

CAMILLE: Just how long is this joke going to continue?

PERDICAN: What joke?

CAMILLE: Your marriage to Rosette.

PERDICAN: Oh, not long, not long. God didn't make us out of iron. Thirty years, forty at most.

CAMILLE: I can't *wait* to dance at your wedding!

PERDICAN: Now, Camille, you mustn't make light of my marriage.

CAMILLE: I'll make whatever I want of it.

PERDICAN: And I'll make my farewell; I've had enough of this.

CAMILLE: Going to see your bride?

PERDICAN: Exactly. That's just where I'm going.

CAMILLE: Give me your arm. I'll go with you.

Rosette enters.

PERDICAN: There you are, my darling! Come. I want to present you to my father.

ROSETTE: My lord, I come to ask you a favor. Everyone I talk to in the village says you love your cousin and you're just courting me as a kind of . . . of joke. A joke to both of you. And they make fun of me when I walk by. And I'll never ever find me a husband in this county 'cause I'm just a laughing stock to everyone. And now, sir, permit me to return this chain and let me go and live in peace with my mum.

CAMILLE: You're a good girl, Rosette. Keep the necklace. It is I who gives it to you now, and my cousin shall have another one from me. As for finding a husband, don't you worry. I'll take it upon myself to find you one.

PERDICAN: That won't be hard; come on, Rosette. I'm taking you to meet my father.

CAMILLE: Why?! It is useless!

PERDICAN: As a matter of fact, you're right. He'll probably behave very badly. Best to let the initial shock wear off. Come with me and we'll take a little stroll through the square. I find it most amusing that they say I don't love you, when I'm about to marry you. By God, we'll show them.

He leaves with Rosette.

CAMILLE: What's happening to me? He just takes her off like that, cool as can be. How strange I feel . . . my head is spinning, and I. . . . Will he really marry her? Really?! . . . Dame Pluche! . . . Dame Pluche! Where is everyone? . . .

A servant enters.

Run after Lord Perdican. Tell him to come back here quickly. I must speak to him.

Servant leaves.

But what then? . . . What's happening to me? . . . I'm

losing hold. I'm losing. . . . My legs feel so weak . . . as if they could no longer . . .

Perdican enters.

Ah!

PERDICAN: You called for me, Camille?

CAMILLE: No . . . no . . .

PERDICAN: Look at you: you're so pale. What do you want? You sent for me. Why? You have something to tell me?

CAMILLE: No. No! . . . Dear God! . . .

She runs to a cross and falls to her knees as the scene transforms itself: all set units vanish except for a stark, bare, rear wall with a small door in it. The cross, perhaps originally part of the architectural design, now stands alone, or hangs above, dominating the scene.

God, my God why have You forsaken me?! You know when I came here I promised to be faithful. You know when I swore to be no man's wife but Thine, I spoke honestly before Thee and my conscience. . . . You *know* that, Heavenly Father, you know that. . . . And will You have no more to do with me now? Oh why have you made truth itself a *liar*? And why am I so weak, why am I so weak? . . . Wretched that I am, I can no longer pray.

PERDICAN: O Pride, thou worst of human counselors, what have you wrought between this girl and me? Look at her there, pale and faint with fear, pressed against the hard, unfeeling stones. She was to have loved me, and we were born for one another. You stopped our mouths just as our hands began to touch.

CAMILLE: Who speaks? . . . Perdican, is it you?

PERDICAN: Mad as we are, we love. What dream is this we've conjured up, Camille? What useless words and miserable imaginings have come between us like a killing wind. Which of us ever meant to hurt the other? Alas, this life's a nightmare foul enough without the devastating dreams we dream alone. Oh God, happiness is rare as a pearl in the deep, and Thou, heavenly Fisher of men, you fetched it up for us from fathoms below, a jewel inestimable, for us to toy with like spoiled children. There was a pathway bringing us together. It had a gentle rise and flowering borders, and it stretched as far as eye could see to find its peace in the horizon. And then of course, came vanity, came anger and confusions, and blocked that path with rocks and cataracts, which should have led to thee, Lord, with a kiss. But we must come to naught for we are mortal. Mortal men and madmen, for we love.

CAMILLE: We love, Perdican. Let me feel it in your heart. This God who sees us cannot be offended. He wishes me to love you. For fifteen years He has known!

PERDICAN: Dear angel, you are my own!

They kiss. A cry is heard from outside.

CAMILLE: That was her voice! Her voice, and then it fell . . .

PERDICAN: I left her on the landing of the stairway. She must have followed me.

CAMILLE: Her cry came from the little balcony. She's been listening!

PERDICAN: What is happening? . . . I can see the blood in
my hands . . .

CAMILLE: Hurry! We must go to her. Oh God, how
cruel! All of it, how cruel!

*She exits by the small door upstage. Perdican remains as if
transfixed.*

PERDICAN: I cannot go with you . . . I feel a paralyzing
fear . . . cold, cold as death. Oh God, I beg you, do
not call murder down upon my head! You see what's
happened here: two unfeeling children, playing with
life and death . . . but our heart is pure . . . this heart
we share is pure! Do not kill Rosette, Just God, do
not! I'll find a husband for her . . . I'll make good all
my fault. . . . She is young and she can be rich, she
can be *happy*. . . . Don't do this, God! Bless us,
instead, your children joined forever. . . . Bless us. . . .
Bless us!!

*Camille reenters. She stands very still, looking straight ahead.
Pause.*

CAMILLE: She is dead. Goodbye, Perdican.

She leaves and closes the door.

Lorenzaccio

TRANSLATED AND ADAPTED BY
PAUL SCHMIDT

The Medici Faction:

Alessandro Medici, the Duke of Florence

Giomo the Hungarian, his bodyguard

Lorenzo Medici (Lorenzaccio)
Cosimo Medici } his cousins

Scoronconcolo, Lorenzo's bodyguard

Maria Soderini, Lorenzo's mother

Caterina Ginori, Lorenzo's cousin

Bindo Altoviti, Lorenzo's uncle

Giuliano Salviati, a dissolute nobleman

Roberto Corsini, Commander of the Citadel

A German Officer

First Court Lady

Second Court Lady

Cardinal Baccio Valori, the Papal Legate

Cardinal Malaspina Cibo

Sior Maurizio, Chairman of the Council of Eight

Guicciardini
Niccolini
Vettori
Capponi } noblemen, members of
Accaiuoli the Council of Eight
Canigiani
Corsi

The Republican Faction:

Marchese Cibo

Marchesa Ricciarda Cibo, his wife

Agnolo, her page

Filippo Strozzi

Piero Strozzi
Tommaso Strozzi
Leo Strozzi, the Prior of Capua } his children
Luisa Strozzi

Palla Ruccellai
Alamanno Salviati } noblemen in favor of the Republic
Francesco Pazzi

Citizens of Florence:

Mondella, a jeweler

A Silk Merchant

Venturi, a silk manufacturer

Tebaldeo, a painter

Maffio

Gabriella, his sister (nonspeaking role)

First Apprentice

Second Apprentice

A Citizen

His Wife

First Tutor

Second Tutor

Strozzi Boy

Salviati Boy

Citizens, exiles, German soldiers, courtiers, guests

PLACE

Florence.

TIME

1 January to 9 January, 1536.

Act One

SCENE ONE

A garden. Moonlight. A house in the distance. Enter the Duke and Lorenzo, wrapped in heavy cloaks; Giomo follows with a lantern.

THE DUKE: If she makes us wait another fifteen minutes, I'm leaving. It's colder than shit out here.

LORENZO: You're the one who was so hot for her, Highness. It will do you good to cool off for a while.

THE DUKE: She was supposed to be leaving her mother's at midnight! It's already after midnight and she still hasn't shown up.

LORENZO: If she doesn't show up, that means I'm a lot more stupid than you thought, and her dear old mother is a lot more honest than I thought.

THE DUKE: And that means there goes a thousand goddam ducats of my money! Well, it was the Pope's money, actually.

LORENZO: Don't worry, I only paid her half in advance. Anyway, trust me. She'll show up. And for a horny pervert like you, what could be better than getting a piece right out of the crib? Believe me, I know these things: one look in those fifteen-year-old eyes and I could see the slut to come!

THE DUKE: Shit, where is she? She was supposed to signal with a light, wasn't she? I can't stay here forever, I'm supposed to go to Nasi's later tonight. It's his masquerade party; I have to make an appearance.

GIOMO: Let's go over by the house, Highness. We're supposed to pick up a girl, she's half paid for already, right? Least we can throw a few rocks at her window.

THE DUKE: This crazy Hungarian has the right idea. Let's go.

They go toward the wing in the distance. Enter Maffio.

MAFFIO: I dreamed I saw my sister here in the garden, wearing diamonds and carrying a lantern. I woke up sweating, it was only a dream. Her bedroom window is closed. In my dream I was crazy with fear, but it's better now. What's that? Who's that, beyond those trees?

Maffio's sister Gabriella crosses in the distance; she carries a lantern, and the moonlight sparkles on a necklace of diamonds.

It's my dream! Gabriella! Gabriella! Where are you going?

Enter the Duke and Giomo.

GIOMO: This must be the brother, walking in his sleep. Lorenzo will take the girl back to the palace, so we're in the clear.

MAFFIO: Hey! Hey you! Hold it! Who are you? *(He draws his sword)*

GIOMO: We are your good friends, you simple peasant.

MAFFIO: What do you want? Where's my sister?

GIOMO: Your sister, my man, has flown the coop. Now be a good friend, and open the garden gate for your betters.

MAFFIO: Get out your sword, you fucker, and fight!

Giomo jumps him and disarms him.

GIOMO: Not so fast, fat-mouth. Drop it, right there.

MAFFIO: Damn you! Damn you! Goddam you! I'll go see the Duke. If there's any law left in Florence, he'll have you arrested and strung up!

GIOMO: You'll go see the Duke?

MAFFIO: Yes, I'll go see the Duke! I know this city is a swamp of muggers and murderers and pimps, but I'm not going to die quiet like the rest of them! If the Duke doesn't know what's going on, here's somebody who's going to let him know! Blood! Blood, goddam you! Give me justice!

GIOMO: Shall I kill him, Highness?

THE DUKE: What? Kill this honest man? Calm down, good friend. Go back to bed. We'll send you a few ducats in the morning. *(He leaves)*

MAFFIO: Alessandro Medici! The Duke!

GIOMO: The Duke in person, my man. And if I were you, I wouldn't go bragging about the great honor he's just done you, dropping by like this, I mean, to visit your sister. You might lose an ear or two. *(He leaves)*

SCENE TWO

A street, just after daybreak. Several people in masquerade costume are leaving a house where the windows are still brightly illuminated. A silk merchant and a jeweler open their shops for the day.

SILK MERCHANT: Hey, Mondella! Feel that wind! It'll blow away all my samples!

JEWELER *(He yawns):* I feel terrible. This masquerade party! I didn't sleep a wink all night.

SILK MERCHANT: My wife neither, friend. Poor thing tossed and turned the whole night. Well, you know how it is when you're young, you want to stay up all night and dance to the music.

JEWELER: Young, young. That's easy for you to say. I'm not young, and that stupid music does *not* make me want to stay up and dance.

Enter two apprentices.

FIRST APPRENTICE: Wait till you see, it's lots of fun. All you have to do is stand close to the door, and you can see them all on their way out, in their costumes and everything. Right here, it's the Nasi house. *(He blows on his fingers)* My hands are freezing.

SECOND APPRENTICE: Are you sure they'll let us do it?

FIRST APPRENTICE: Who's got the right to stop us? We're citizens of Florence! You'll catch on, all you have to do is notice their clothes, and later on at work you can say, oh, I'm so tired, I was up all night at a party, at Prince Aldobrandini's, and then you tell them what the Prince had on, and it's no lie, so they have to believe you! Come on, let's go.

They move off toward the door of the house.

JEWELER: Did you hear those little hustlers? I hope I never catch one of my apprentices trying a trick like that.

SILK MERCHANT: Now, now, Mondella. That's just the way young people are. God, I used to be just like them, out sniffing the night air, looking for a little excitement. Will you look at the costumes on some of the nobles! By God, that's my silk they're dancing in, all those good-looking rich people with their fancy names.

JEWELER: There's more than one of those silk dresses that isn't paid for yet, neighbor, you know it as well as I do. Let the Duke and the court have themselves a good time; that's about all they know how to do.

SILK MERCHANT: Just what do you mean by that, Mondella?

JEWELER: I'm talking about things like the cases and cases of wine that get delivered to the court. What's the good of drinking like that, getting yourself drunk every night? Nothing pleasant about that. God doesn't like it, either.

SILK MERCHANT: I have to admit, Carnival got a little out of hand this year. Their damn street football game ran right through my display, I lost fifty florins worth of fabric. Thank God the Strozzis paid me for it.

JEWELER: The Strozzis! Good for them! Best man in all Florence, Filippo Strozzi.

SILK MERCHANT: That may be, but it didn't stop his boy Piero from running his football right through my display. Still, God bless the Duke, I say. The court is good for business.

JEWELER: The court is built on our backs, I tell you!
There was a time, not so long ago either, the city of
Florence was like a decent, well-built house, and the
palaces of our noble families were the columns that
held it up. But then one day two crazy architects
thought it would be a good idea to remodel, I mean
the Pope and the Emperor, and they smashed through
a wall in order to get themselves in. Then they took
one of those columns I was telling you about, the
Medicis to be exact, and decided to make them into a
tower, and they built them a pile of mud and slime
they call the Citadel. And now that Citadel is full of
German guards, they sit there gambling and drinking
and spying on all of us! The Medicis run this city
because they have those Germans in the Citadel!
That's the reason we have a Duke who's the Pope's
bastard, a punk who should have been a butcher boy
or a truck driver, and he sleeps with our daughters,
he drinks up our wine, he breaks our shop windows,
and on top of it all he gets a salary for doing it. And
we pay him!

SILK MERCHANT: Christ! Let me tell you, Mondella,
you're my neighbor and I like you, but I wouldn't go
around talking like that to everyone you meet.

JEWELER: What can they do? Banish me like the rest? I
can live in Rome just as well as here. The hell with
them all, them and their masquerades!

*He goes into his shop. The silk merchant joins the crowd of
bystanders. A citizen passes with his wife.*

WIFE: The whole place is lit up! They're still dancing at

this hour! Now that's what I call a party! Someone
told me the Duke was there.

CITIZEN: Fine thing, turning day into night and night
into day. My God, will you look at that! Armed
guards at a masquerade party! What are things in this
town coming to? It's all those damn Germans.

WIFE: Oh, look over there! What a fantastic dress! It must
have cost a fortune. Maybe someday I'll have enough
for a dress like that . . .

They leave.

A SOLDIER *(To the silk merchant):* Out of the way, scum!
Watch out for the horses!

SILK MERCHANT: Watch who you call scum, you dumb
German!

The soldier hits him with his stick.

Is this your idea of a peace treaty? You can't treat
honest citizens like this!

FIRST APPRENTICE: See over there? The one that just
took off his mask? That's Palla Ruccellai, he's a real
nobleman! And that short one next to him, that's
Tommaso Strozzi, the one they call Masaccio.

A PAGE *(He shouts):* The Duke's horse!

SECOND APPRENTICE: We should go, that's the Duke
coming.

FIRST APPRENTICE: What's the matter, you think he's
going to eat you?

A crowd begins to grow around the gate.

FIRST APPRENTICE: That's Niccolini. And that one is Corsini, the Commander of the Citadel.

The Duke leaves the house, together with Giuliano Salviati. Both are dressed in nuns' habits and wear masks.

THE DUKE *(He mounts his horse)*: You coming, Giuliano?
SALVIATI: Not yet, Highness. *(He whispers something)*
THE DUKE: It sounds hot! Good luck!
SALVIATI: She's beautiful, and she's mine! . . . If I can just get rid of my wife! *(He goes back to the party)*
THE DUKE *(He laughs)*: Salviati, you're drunk. By Christ, you're walking at an angle!

He leaves with his attendants.

FIRST APPRENTICE: It'll all be over in a minute, now that the Duke's gone.

Guests in costume leave in all directions.

SECOND APPRENTICE: Pink, green, blue, I can't believe all the colors! This must be heaven!
A CITIZEN: This party must have been going on for days. Look at those two, they can barely stand up.

The Commander mounts his horse: someone throws a broken bottle that hits him on the shoulder.

COMMANDER: All right, by God, who did that?
A GUEST IN COSTUME: Can't you guess, Corsini? Look up at the window! It's Lorenzaccio, all dressed up like a nun!

COMMANDER: Goddam you, Lorenzo, you hurt my horse. *(The window slams shut)* Goddam drunk! I'm sick and tired of your stupid jokes! Goddam little faggot never smiled twice in his life, but he plays more tricks than a drunken college boy. *(He leaves)*

Luisa Strozzi comes out of Nasi's house, accompanied by Giuliano Salviati: he holds her stirrup. She mounts up. A valet and a governess follow her.

GIULIANO: What a pretty leg you've got, baby! You're a sunbean that burns me to the bone!

LUISA: Sir, that's no way for a gentleman to talk.

GIULIANO: What pretty eyes you've got, baby! What beautiful shoulders, all soft and sweaty! What I wouldn't give to tuck you in tonight, baby! I could take off your stockings real slow.

LUISA: Let go my foot, Salviati.

GIULIANO: No, by God, not till you tell me you'll go to bed with me.

Luisa whips her horse and gallops off.

A GUEST IN COSTUME *(To Giuliano)*: She went off like a shot. I'm afraid you made her a very angry lady, Salviati.

GIULIANO: An angry lady and a cold morning. . . . *Basta!* *(He leaves)*

SCENE THREE

The Cibo palace. The Marchese in traveling clothes, the Marchesa, Cardinal Cibo.

MARCHESA: Goodbye, my darling. Come back soon!

CARDINAL: Aren't your tears overdoing it a bit, Marchesa? One would think my brother was leaving for the Holy Land. I don't think he runs much risk going off to his own farm.

THE MARCHESE: Her tears are beautiful, brother. Don't speak badly of them. *(He kisses his wife)*

CARDINAL: It's just that I hate to see virtue always with a tear-stained face.

MARCHESA: Why, my lord Cardinal? Shouldn't virtue be allowed to cry? Are tears reserved only for sorrow or fear?

THE MARCHESE: God, no! The best tears in the world are lovers' tears. Look at mine. Now, darling, any messages for your fountains and gardens?

MARCHESA: My gardens! Oh, darling, take me with you!

THE MARCHESE: Oh, you don't want to go dragging through the fields with me. I'll be working with the farmers, clearing woods and plowing, we'll all be full of mud. But I promise you, the first flower I see, I'll drop everything and come get you.

MARCHESA: The first flower in our garden is always the one I love most. Winter seems so long! I always start thinking the flowers will never come back.

The Marchese leaves. The Marchesa is alone with the Cardinal. There is a silence.

CARDINAL: Wasn't it today you wanted me to hear your confession, Marchesa?

MARCHESA: I'd like to wait, Cardinal, if you don't mind. Let's do it this evening, if Your Eminence is free, or tomorrow, whatever suits you. My time just now isn't my own. *(She goes to the window and waves to her husband)*

CARDINAL: If a faithful servant of the Almighty were allowed any regrets, I think I might envy my brother. So simple, so easy, just a short trip to the country, and such delicious sadness at his going! A happy man, whose wife is still in love with him after seven years of marriage! It is seven years, Marchesa, isn't it?

MARCHESA: Yes, Cardinal, it is. Seven years. My son is just six.

CARDINAL: Were you at the Nasis masquerade party?

MARCHESA: Yes, Cardinal, I was.

CARDINAL: And the Duke was dressed as a nun?

MARCHESA: Oh? Was the Duke dressed as a nun?

CARDINAL: Someone told me he went dressed as a nun; but they might have been joking.

MARCHESA: No, they were quite right, he was. Ah, Malaspina, we live in an age when sanctity is not taken seriously.

CARDINAL: It's quite possible to take sanctity seriously and still go to a costume party dressed as a nun. That doesn't necessarily indicate any deep hostility to the Catholic Church.

MARCHESA: It's the example that disturbs me, not his intentions. I'm not as blasé as you; I must admit I was shocked. Of course I'm always rather vague about what is and what isn't permitted according to your mysterious rules of conduct. God only knows what they lead to, eventually.

CARDINAL: Oh, don't be so serious, Marchesa! The Duke is young! He probably made a ravishing nun. Didn't he?

MARCHESA: Oh, very attractive, he looked a lot like his queer cousin Ippolito.

CARDINAL: My, my, quite the little freedom fighter, aren't we, my dear? How everyone hates the poor Duke!

MARCHESA: And you, working as his right-hand man! How can you? How can you bear that the Duke of Florence was appointed by the German Emperor Charles the Fifth, that he is nothing but a political henchman of the Pope? You are my husband's youngest brother! How can you bear to see the sun set over Florence behind a Citadel built by Germans? How can you stand it that everyone in this administration is in the pay of the Emperor? That corruption is pimping us into slavery? You priests! How can you? *(She leaves)*

The Cardinal is alone. He goes to a tapestry, draws it aside, and calls in a low voice.

CARDINAL: Agnolo!

A page enters.

Anything new today?

AGNOLO: This letter, Eminence.

CARDINAL: Give it to me.

AGNOLO: But Eminence, that's a sin!

CARDINAL: Nothing is a sin when you obey the orders of a priest.

Agnolo gives him the letter.

Quite a scene, I must say, to see how angry our dear Marchesa can get, just before she runs off to a romantic rendezvous with the tyrant she claims she hates! And her cheeks still wet with Republican tears! *(He opens the letter and reads it)* "Either you agree to belong to me, or you bring disaster on me, on you, on your entire family." The Duke always comes to the point, I must say. But does the Marchesa believe him, that's what I cannot figure out. It's two months now that he's been in hot pursuit; for Alessandro, that's a long time. It must surely be enough for Ricciarda Cibo. *(He gives the letter back to the page)* Put this back where you found it. This is just between you and me, isn't it? And I'll take care of you, won't I? Remember that.

He gives the page his hand to kiss and leaves.

SCENE FOUR

A room in the Duke's palace. Duke Alessandro stands at the balcony window, watching two pages work out a horse in the courtyard below. Enter Cardinal Valori and Sior Maurizio.

THE DUKE *(To Valori)*: Your Eminence had messages from Rome this morning, no? From the Pope?
VALORI: Paul the Third sends his blessing to Your

Highness, and all best wishes for your continued
health and happiness.

THE DUKE: Best wishes? Is that all, Valori?

VALORI: His Holiness worries that Your Highness may be
creating new dangers for yourself because of your—
how shall we say—excessive indulgence. The people
of Florence are not used to a ruler who behaves like a
dictator, and the Emperor, on his last visit, told you
that quite specifically.

THE DUKE: Goddam, that horse is beautiful! Look, Sior
Maurizio, look at his chest!

SIOR MAURIZIO: A superb animal, Highness.

THE DUKE: All right, all right, Valori, let's have it. Get to
the bad part. The Emperor and the Pope may have
made me a Duke, but by God what they put in my
hand was not a scepter, it's a hatchet. And everybody
for a hundred miles around knows it's a hatchet. So
come on, what else did the Pope say?

VALORI: Highness, I am a priest. It is my duty to repeat
to you what I have been told; if you mean to interpret
it in a bad light, my feelings will keep me from saying
a word more.

THE DUKE: That's all you have to say?

SIOR MAURIZIO: May I speak plainly, Highess? I think
we can clear this up fairly simply.

THE DUKE: Well?

SIOR MAURIZIO: The Pope is angry because of what has
been going on here at court.

THE DUKE: What's that supposed to mean?

SIOR MAURIZIO: I said at court, Highness. It has nothing
to do with you personally. You are responsible for
your own actions. But the Pope wants Lorenzo

Medici arrested and sent to Rome. He is a fugitive from the Pope's justice.

THE DUKE: From the Pope's justice? So far as I know, the only Pope Lorenzo ever insulted was my dear dead father Clement the Seventh, and I hope he rots in hell right this minute.

SIOR MAURIZIO: Clement the Seventh allowed that juvenile delinquent to escape from Rome after he had gotten drunk and knocked the heads off all the statues on the Arch of Constantine. Paul the Third has not forgotten the incident. He wants to make an example of him, as a titled ringleader of moral corruption and decay here in Florence.

THE DUKE: Oh for Chrissake, can't the Pope take a joke? If moral corruption and decay bothers him so much, why doesn't he do something about his bastard son Piero, him and his boyfriend, the Bishop of Fano? They always drag up those fucking statues to try to get back at poor Renzo. I don't see why the Pope gets so worked up; if those statues came to life today he'd excommunicate them tomorrow.

SIOR MAURIZIO: Lorenzo is an atheist. He makes a joke out of everything. If Your Highness' government does not have the respect of all your people, it will never get onto a firm footing. The people call Lorenzo Lorenzaccio. They know he arranges your parties and your . . . late-night amusements, and that's enough for them.

THE DUKE: And that's enough out of you! You forget Lorenzo is my cousin.

Enter Cardinal Cibo.

Cardinal, listen to these gentlemen. They tell me the Pope is shocked by poor Renzo's behavior, and they say he's the scandal of my administration.

CARDINAL: Francesco Molza, I believe, has just made a speech before the Roman Academy, protesting the desecration of the Arch of Constantine. It was a speech in Latin, too, as I recall.

THE DUKE: Oh for godsake, all of you, you piss me off. What are you afraid of Renzo for? He's a coward, a crybaby, a faggot, he tries to act tough and he hasn't got the nerve! Why do you think he never wears a sword? He's afraid he might see his own shadow! He wants to be a philosopher and he can't think for shit, he wants to be a poet and he can't write for shit. No, goddam it! I don't scare like the rest of you! They can write all the fucking Latin speeches they want, they can say what they want, Lorenzo is my baby and I like him and by Christ he stays right here.

CARDINAL: If I were afraid of him, Highness, it wouldn't be for the sake of your court, or of Florence. It would be because of you.

THE DUKE: Is that supposed to be a joke? Come here a minute, I'll tell you the truth. *(He talks in a low voice to the Cardinal)* Everything I know about the bastards I banish, everything I find out about these fucking plots to restore the Republic, I get from Lorenzo. He's slippery, like an eel; he gets in everywhere and tells me everything. He's the one who keeps in touch with all those goddam Strozzis. Of course he's my pimp; do you expect me to pimp for myself? But if anybody gets into trouble, it's not going to be me. Look!

Lorenzo enters at a distance, from the courtyard below.

Look at him! He's a walking hangover! Look at that skinny butt, look at those limp wrists, look at the circles under his eyes. He hasn't even got the strength to laugh; all he can do is smile like a girl. What can you see in him to be afraid of? You're all crazy! Hey! Renzo! Come on up here, Sior Maurizio wants to pick a fight with you!

LORENZO: Well, all my cousin's friends. Good morning, gentlemen.

THE DUKE: Lorenzo, listen to this. We've been talking about you for the last fifteen minutes. Guess what? You've just been excommunicated in Latin, baby, and Sior Maurizio here thinks you're a dangerous criminal. So does the Cardinal. And good old Valori is too good even to mention your name.

LORENZO: Me dangerous, Eminence? Who for? The saints in heaven or the whores of Florence?

CARDINAL: A high-class bitch bites just as bad as a bitch in the street.

LORENZO: I thought priests made all their insults in Latin.

SIOR MAURIZIO: He made it in plain everyday language so you could understand it.

LORENZO: Oh, Sior Maurizio. I didn't recognize you! Perhaps because you're wearing a clean shirt for a change. Cousin, the next time you're finished with one of your downtown hookers, send her over to Sior Maurizio. A man his age shouldn't live without a woman, especially a gorilla too ugly to get one for himself.

SIOR MAURIZIO: You make that kind of joke, you'd better know how to defend yourself. If I were you, now, I'd look around for a sword.

LORENZO: Whoever told you I was a fighter made a big

mistake; I'm just a poor student of the liberal arts.

SIOR MAURIZIO: Your jokes have sharp points; that makes them dangerous weapons. But they're not a man's weapon; a man uses something else. *(He draws his sword)*

VALORI: You cannot draw your sword in front of the Duke!

THE DUKE *(He laughs)*: Let him alone, let him alone. All right, Renzo, this is it! I'll be your second. Somebody give him a sword!

LORENZO: Highness! What do you mean?

THE DUKE: Hey! What happened to your funny stories all of a sudden? What's the matter, cousin, why are you shaking? Come on, you're a disgrace to the name of Medici! I'm only a bastard, but I'm a better Medici than you are, and you're supposed to be legitimate! Get him a sword, somebody get him a sword! You can't insult a Medici like that and get away with it. You pages, get up here, I want the whole court out here, I want the whole goddam city to see this!

LORENZO: Highness, you're making fun of me!

THE DUKE: It was fun five minutes ago, now it's serious! You make me ashamed! Get him a sword!

Pages and courtiers enter; the Duke grabs a sword from a page and offers it to Lorenzo.

VALORI: Your Highness, this is going too far. Drawing a sword in Your Highess' presence is a crime, but it's a crime that can be dealt with in private, not in front of the whole court!

THE DUKE: Don't you dare talk when I'm talking!

VALORI: I'm sure Your Highness was only trying to make

a joke, and I'm sure that Sior Maurizio had the same idea.

THE DUKE: And you think it still isn't a joke? Who the hell thinks this is serious? Look at Renzo, for godsakes, he's pale, he's shaking, look at his face! Christ, he's going to faint!

Lorenzo staggers and slips to the ground. The Duke laughs.

See? What did I tell you? I told you what would happen. All he has to do is look at a sword and he faints like a girl! All right, sweetie, that's enough. Somebody take him home to his mama.

The pages carry Lorenzo out.

SIOR MAURIZIO: That cowardly sonofabitch!
THE DUKE: Maurizio, you shut up! You watch what you say, you hear me? You don't say things like that about him when I'm around!
VALORI: Poor boy!

The crowd disperses; Valori and Sior Maurizio leave; Cardinal Cibo remains alone with the Duke.

CARDINAL: Can you believe his behavior, Highness?
THE DUKE: Of course I believe it. Do you really think a Medici would let himself be insulted in public as a joke? Anyway, it's not the first time. He gets that way every time he sees a sword.

SCENE FIVE

A street in front of a church. The jeweler and the silk merchant in front of their shops, a trattoria with tables and chairs. A crowd of people leaving the church; among them noblemen, citizens, and two ladies of the court accompanied by a German officer.

FIRST LADY OF THE COURT *(To second lady)*: What an inspiring sermon! And did I tell you he's my daughter's confessor?

They pass a shop window.

That white and gold would look marvellous for evening, but my dear, however would you keep it clean?

Two noblemen stop by the jeweler's shop.

JEWELER *(To the noblemen)*: That Citadel! The people of Florence will never put up with it. To wake up one morning and see that Tower of Babel sticking up into the air, like a huge slum! These Germans will never take root in Florence, but it will take a heavy hoe to dig them out.

SILK MERCHANT: Good morning, ladies! Right over here! Here's a lovely place in the shade.

A NOBLEMAN: You come from an old Florentine family, Mondella. You hate these dictators, I can tell. I can see your hands shake as you sit there carving your silver.

JEWELER: You are very perceptive, Excellency. I do hate them. I suppose if I were a great artist, now, I might think differently. A great artist can't afford patriotism;

he gets his commissions from the men who have the power and money. But all I make are trinkets.

Two citizens sit at a table at the trattoria.

FIRST CITIZEN: There was a riot yesterday?

SECOND CITIZEN: Nothing serious. Two young men killed in the old marketplace.

FIRST CITIZEN: What a terrible thing for their families.

SECOND CITIZEN: What do you expect? What are decent young people supposed to do with a government like this? The Pope and the Emperor have gotten together and produced a dictator for us, a bastard who has the power of life and death over every one of us, and he doesn't even know his own mother's name.

JEWELER *(Coming up to them)*: You talk like patriots, friends. I'd be more careful if I were you. Especially around the thug heading this way.

The German officer and the two ladies of the court approach.

GERMAN OFFICER: You men. Out. These ladies want to sit.

The citizens move to another table; the ladies of the court sit down. The silk merchant follows with his samples.

FIRST LADY: This is Venetian?

SILK MERCHANT: Yes, lady. Shall I measure a few yards for you?

FIRST LADY: Yes, do, please. Isn't that Giuliano Salviati who just went by?

GERMAN OFFICER: Yes. That's him now, walking back

and forth in front of the church. He is a real man!

SECOND LADY: He's a very rude man. I'd like to see some of your silk stockings.

GERMAN OFFICER: He has none small enough for your little feet.

FIRST LADY: Oh, you and your compliments. If that's really Salviati, go tell him I want to talk to him.

GERMAN OFFICER: I get him. *(He leaves)*

FIRST LADY: He does everything you tell him, that German of yours. What else does he do, I wonder?

SECOND LADY: Believe me, darling, it's been a long time since anyone's done what he does to me!

They leave. Enter Leo Strozzi, the Prior of Capua.

THE PRIOR: I'll have a glass of lemonade, please, if you don't mind. *(He sits down)*

FIRST CITIZEN: That's Leo Strozzi, the Prior of Capua. He's a real patriot!

THE PRIOR: Were you in church today, gentlemen? What did you think of the sermon?

FIRST CITIZEN: Very beautiful, Your Reverence.

SECOND CITIZEN *(To the jeweler)*: It's no wonder everyone loves the Strozzi family, they're not proud people. Look, I like that; he's a nobleman, but he talks to his neighbor just like the next man.

THE PRIOR: I'll tell you frankly, I thought the sermon was a little too beautiful. I don't think a good sermon has to make the stained glass rattle. I do some preaching from time to time, and if I can bring tears to the eyes of decent men, that's when I feel I've done my job.

Enter Salviati; he sits at another table.

SALVIATI: Now that's what I call a good-looking woman, over there. Where the hell do I know her from? Oh, right, I remember. I spent the night with her last week.

THE PRIOR *(To the citizens)*: Weren't you one of the men who signed a petition to the Duke?

FIRST CITIZEN: I was, and I'm not ashamed to say it. It was a petition for the exiles.

THE PRIOR: Do you have any in your family?

FIRST CITIZEN: Two, Excellency, my father and my uncle. I'm the only man left at home.

SECOND CITIZEN: That Salviati has a dirty mouth.

JEWELER: What do you expect, a man like that? He's gone through most of his money, he lives on what he gets because he hangs around with those Medicis! And his wife! The worst reputation in the city! He talks about every woman he meets the way other people talk about his wife.

SALVIATI: Isn't that Luisa Strozzi crossing the street?

SILK MERCHANT: It is, Excellency. I know most of the noble ladies of Florence by sight. If I'm not mistaken, the girl with her is her younger sister.

SALVIATI: You're right, that's Luisa. I met her the other night at the masquerade party at Nasi's. By God, I remember now, she has great legs. I'm going to make it with her one of these days.

THE PRIOR *(He turns around)*: What do you mean by that?

SALVIATI: Just what I said. Anyway, it was her idea. I was just trying to be polite, and by mistake I got a hand on her leg, that's all it took!

THE PRIOR: Giuliano, you may not know this, but you are talking about my sister.

SALVIATI: I know who I'm talking about. But all women are made for men, so why can't I screw your sister?

THE PRIOR *(He stands)*: Friend, I owe you for a glass of lemonade. *(He puts a coin on the table and leaves)*

SALVIATI: Now there's a man I admire. One little remark about his sister and he forgets his change.

The prior stops and looks back at him.

Go on, make a face, you don't scare me!

SCENE SIX

The banks of the Arno River, early evening. Enter Caterina and Maria.

CATERINA: The sun is starting to set. How strange! Here by the river, the noises of the city seem far away. All that frenzy becomes another of the sounds of nature.

MARIA: We should be getting back. Wrap your scarf around your neck.

CATERINA: Let's not go just yet—unless you're getting cold. Look, dear, what a beautiful sky! How vast and serene! It makes me feel the presence of the Almighty. Why do you look away? Something's upset you; you've been like this all day.

MARIA: Not upset, I've been in pain. Haven't you heard the story everyone is telling about Lorenzo? He's the laughingstock of Florence.

CATERINA: Dear, cowardice isn't a crime. And bravery isn't always a virtue. Why should people laugh at weakness? It's a privilege to be able to act the way you feel.

MARIA: Could you love a man who was full of fear? You

see, Caterina, you blush. Lorenzo is your cousin, but
if he were someone else's cousin, how would you feel?

CATERINA: I know, it's sad. But that isn't really what
bothers me most about him. He may not have the
courage of a Medici, but the worst part is, he . . . he
has absolutely no morals anymore.

MARIA: Caterina, don't let's talk about it. *(Pause)* What a
terrible thing for a mother, not to be able to talk
about her son.

CATERINA: And it's all the fault of Florence! It's here he
went wrong! You know what he used to be like,
growing up, he was so hopeful, so full of ambition.
. . . Even today I keep hoping that something will
change, that all of that isn't totally dead.

MARIA: I sometimes think he's fallen into a bottomless
pit. All that talent, such a sensitive boy, and he had
such a love for the truth!

CATERINA: Don't take it so hard.

MARIA: I said I didn't want to talk about him, and here I
am talking about nothing else. Oh, Caterina, he isn't
even as handsome as he was. He never smiles
anymore, he only sneers. He trusts no one.

CATERINA: Sometimes I find his strange melancholy even
more attractive.

MARIA: He was born to be a prince, to sit on a throne!
Didn't I have a right to see that happen? Oh, Cattina,
how hard it is to see the face of a monster who still
calls you Mother!

CATERINA: It's getting dark. How still it is! Let's go
back, Maria, the roads are full of exiles, they scare me.

MARIA: This is more of Lorenzo's work! There's not a
single one of these decent people, family men, that
my son hasn't betrayed. All the citizens who want to

restore the Republic still trust him, because he bears the name of their great protector; if they only knew! He shows all their letters to the Duke! But still they trust him. Even the Strozzi. Poor Filippo! What a sad old age my son will cost him!

CATERINA: Come, dear. You mustn't cry.

They leave. The sun has almost set. A group of exiles begins to gather.

FIRST EXILE: Where will you go?

SECOND EXILE: To Pisa. What about you?

FIRST EXILE: To Rome.

THIRD EXILE: I'm going to Venice, and our friends here are going to Ferrara. What will happen to us all, so far away from one another?

FOURTH EXILE: Goodbye, neighbor. Let's hope we meet again, in better times.

FIFTH EXILE: Goodbye. You and I can go part of the way together, as far as Our Lady's shrine.

He begins to leave with fourth exile. Enter Maffio.

FIRST EXILE: Maffio, is that you? What are you doing here?

MAFFIO: I'm one of you now. You know the Duke kidnapped my sister. I tried to protect her; the Duke's bodyguard jumped me and took my sword away. Next day I received a court order telling me to leave the city. It was delivered with a bagful of money.

SECOND EXILE: Where's your sister now?

MAFFIO: I saw her last night, coming out of the theatre.

She was . . . she was wearing a lot of very expensive jewelry. God help her.

THIRD EXILE: I hope they all sink in their own shit. Then we can die happy.

FOURTH EXILE: I had a letter from Filippo Strozzi. He says it won't be long before we have an army at our command.

THIRD EXILE: Thank God for Filippo! As long as he's alive, freedom in Italy isn't dead!

The group begins to separate; the exiles embrace, and look back at the city.

FIRST EXILE: Goodbye, Florence. Goodbye to the stinking hole of Italy.

SECOND EXILE: Goodbye to a breast gone dry; Florence has no more milk for her own children.

THIRD EXILE: Goodbye, Florence. Goodbye to the bastard bones of a great country.

FOURTH EXILE: Goodbye to a stinking swamp with no name.

ALL THE EXILES: Goodbye, Florence! Die, Florence! God curse you, Florence! Curse your women! Curse the milk in your babies' mouths! Curse your crying! Curse your prayers, curse the bread you eat, curse the air you breathe! Curse the last rotten drop of blood in your veins!

SCENE SEVEN

The Strozzi palace. Filippo alone in his study.

FILIPPO: Ten citizens in exile from our neighborhood
　　alone. Young Maffio exiled, and his sister become a
　　kept woman overnight. Poor child! Is corruption a law
　　of nature, then? Is virtue only something you wear to
　　church on Sundays? It's hard enough to think that
　　human happiness may be only a dream, but that evil
　　should be eternal, irrevocable, impossible to change—
　　No. I cannot accept that. A philosopher must work for
　　the good of all mankind!

　　　　But how easy it is, here at a desk, to makes lines on a
　　page, blueprints for happiness . . . and how hard it is,
　　with this old hand, to lift the first stone and set it in
　　place!

　　　　Act! We must act, and act boldly! The Republic.
　　There's the word we need. Even if it is still only a
　　word, it means something, something real, because
　　people rise up when they hear it spoken . . .

　　　　Is that you, Piero? Come in, will you, I want to talk to
　　you.

Enter Piero Strozzi and the Prior of Capua.

　　Ah, Leo! How was your day?

THE PRIOR: It was quite pleasant, except for one rather
　　disagreeable incident that . . . that took me awhile to
　　get over.

PIERO: What happened?

THE PRIOR: You see, I stopped to have a glass of
　　lemonade. . . . No, forget it. It was a stupid accident.

FILIPPO: What is it? What's the matter with you? You look like a soul in torment.

THE PRIOR: It's nothing, just a stupid remark, that's all. It doesn't mean a thing.

PIERO: What do you mean, a remark? About who? About you?

THE PRIOR: No, not about me exactly. I don't care what people say about me.

PIERO: Well who then? Talk, for godsake!

THE PRIOR: Look, I was wrong to mention it. There's no point in getting upset by anything a man like Salviati says . . .

PIERO: Salviati? That sonofabitch! What did he say?

THE PRIOR: You're right, he's an animal. Look, it's all over, I don't want to think about it anymore.

PIERO: Well, I want you to think about it and tell me what he said! I want an excuse to kick that bastard's brains out! Who did he talk about? Us? Father? Christ, I hate that Salviati! You tell me what he said, you hear me?

THE PRIOR: He said something, in this shop, right in front of me, something . . . really offensive about our sister.

PIERO: Oh God. What did he say? Come on, tell me!

THE PRIOR: It was something vulgar.

PIERO: Goddam you, priest! You see I'm crazy already, and you make me crazier! Just say exactly what it was he said! A word is a word, God won't damn you for it.

FILIPPO: Piero! Piero! Show more respect for your brother!

THE PRIOR: He said he was going to screw her, that was the word he used, and that she said she'd let him.

PIERO: He was going to scr—. Oh, Christ! Oh, Jesus

Jesus Christ! What time is it? Tell me the time!

FILIPPO: The time? You're ready to explode!

Piero draws his sword.

You put that away! What do you want with a sword in the house?

PIERO: I don't want anything with it. See? It's dinnertime, isn't it? Time for dinner? Let's just go have dinner. All right?

They leave.

SCENE EIGHT

The steps of a church. Tebaldeo is sketching. Enter Lorenzo and Cardinal Valori.

VALORI: But why won't the Duke go to church? Believe me, there is no greater satisfaction than the beauty of the Catholic mass! What artist could find a more perfect model for Paradise? It offers something for everyone: organ music, the splendid vestments, paintings by the greatest of our painters, the perfume of incense, the silver voices of the choir—

LORENZO: I agree. Everything you say is absolutely true. It's also absolutely false, like everything else in this world.

TEBALDEO *(He approaches Valori)*: Excuse me, Your Eminence, I couldn't help overhearing you, and I too agree with everything you say. I'm an ordinary man, but I too have felt that divine beauty.

VALORI: Aren't you that young painter? Freccia?

TEBALDEO: Not much of a painter, really. I love art better than I'm able to make it. But I spend a lot of time in church, and that's where my love of art comes from. The beautiful paintings of Raphael and Michelangelo —it's in church that you really understand them. For me, art is a religion.

LORENZO: Isn't that a canvas you're holding right now? Let's see it.

TEBALDEO: Oh, I couldn't show this to such great connoisseurs. It's just a small sketch of a great dream.

LORENZO: You paint your dreams? I'd like to have you paint a few of mine.

TEBALDEO: But that's what art is all about, bringing dreams to life. *(He shows them his painting)*

VALORI: Well, that's very nice . . . not exactly a master-piece—but why would I want to compliment a man who's so modest himself? You're still practically a boy, aren't you?

LORENZO: What is it, a portrait or a landscape? Maybe I'm looking at it upside down; should I turn it the other way?

TEBALDEO: Excellency, you're making fun of me. It's a view of the graveyard behind the church.

LORENZO: Oh, I see. So it's about the mortality of men and the immortality of art, is that it?

VALORI: You shouldn't make fun of the boy. Look, you've hurt his pride. *(To Tebaldeo)* Why not come visit me sometime? And bring some more of your work, I'd like to see it. *(He exits)*

LORENZO: Why don't you come visit me? I'll invite La Mazzafirra and you can paint her naked.

TEBALDEO: I respect my art too much to paint a whore.

LORENZO: God took the trouble to create her; you at
       least could take the trouble to paint her. What about
       a landscape? Will you paint me a view of Florence?

TEBALDEO: Oh course, Excellency.

LORENZO: How would you go about it?

TEBALDEO: From the east. I'd set up my easel on the left
       bank of the Arno. That's the widest and most
       beautiful view of the whole city.

LORENZO: You'd paint the whole city? Streets, houses,
       public places, everything?

TEBALDEO: Yes, Excellency.

LORENZO: If you're willing to paint a whorehouse, why
       not paint a whore?

TEBALDEO: That's not the way I was taught to talk about
       my mother.

LORENZO: What do you mean, your mother?

TEBALDEO: Florence is my mother, Excellency, my
       motherland.

LORENZO: Then that makes you a bastard, because your
       mother's a whore.

TEBALDEO: The blood of my motherland waters a magic
       plant that cures all ills. That plant is art, and
       sometimes art needs corruption as a kind of fertilizer.

LORENZO: What the fuck is that supposed to mean?

TEBALDEO: Other countries may be happy and peaceful,
       but they don't always produce great art. Inspiration is
       the brother of suffering.

LORENZO: Miserable people make great artists, you
       mean? Jesus, I like the way your mind works! Families
       can suffer and nations can die of starvation, and it
       fills you with inspiration! That's wonderful!

TEBALDEO: I don't laugh at suffering. All I'm saying is

that art is a kind of suffering too, close to other
sufferings.

LORENZO: And you really prefer being poor? You
wouldn't mind starving? Your jacket is worn out.
Would you wear a new one, if I gave it to you—one
with my name on it?

TEBALDEO: I don't belong to anybody. If you want your
mind to be free, then your body has to be free too.

LORENZO: You know what I feel like right now? Calling
out my boys and having them beat the shit out of you.

TEBALDEO: Why?

LORENZO: Because I can do it. *(Pause)* You must be crazy
to stay in a city where someone like me, a Medici
playboy, can beat the shit out of you to celebrate your
idea of being free, and there's not a goddam thing
you can do about it.

TEBALDEO: Florence is my mother and I love her. That's
why I stay here. I'm not stupid. I know how this city
is run. That's why I always carry a knife.

LORENZO: What would you do if the Duke came up to
you and tried to kill you? Just like that, for fun? He
does that, you know, he kills people for fun. Would
you kill him?

TEBALDEO: If he tried to kill me, I'd kill him.

LORENZO: You dare tell *me* that?

TEBALDEO: Why not? Why should you care about me? I
don't hurt you, I don't hurt anybody. I spend the day
in my studio. Sundays I go to church. I sing in the
choir. People say I have a nice voice, and sometimes I
even get a little solo. Nights I spend with my
girlfriend. If it's a nice night we sleep up on the roof.
Nobody knows me, and I don't know anybody. I leave

people alone. What difference does it make to anybody whether I'm alive or dead?

LORENZO: And do you believe in the Republic? Or do you love being ruled by a dictator?

TEBALDEO: I'm an artist. I love my mother and my girlfriend.

LORENZO: You come see me tomorrow. I want you to paint me a big painting. I need it as a wedding present.

SCENE NINE

The Cibo palace. Cardinal Cibo, alone, paces near a prie-dieu.

CARDINAL: I follow your orders, Holy Father. Your papal legate is an honest man, but nothing hinders me. I can poke around in slippery places he doesn't dare walk on. You knew what you were doing when you sent me here to Florence, without any official position to annoy Alessandro. Let him hate his authority figures; he'll always come to me for advice. Your secret agent? Oh, yes—your secret agent, and I shall be the iron chain that keeps him helpless. One end of that chain is in the Emperor's hands and the other, Pope, is in yours. That's what you expect me to do, and that's what I will do. And the only tool I need is right here in this house. Alessandro loves my sister-in-law. I assume she's flattered. His love is a doubtful proposition, but I know her fantasy, I know what she thinks she's capable of, and that's where I can use her exactly to my advantage. Who knows what influence an intelligent woman can have over a man, even a pig like the Duke? And what a temptation, Ricciarda! The sin is not without a certain pleasure, and for such a glorious cause! To hold that young lion in your arms, weep as you talk to him about the sorrows of the motherland, try to strike a divine spark from that rough rock—oh, it's well worth a little adultery, isn't it? You could save Florence! And if you lose a husband in the process, destroy his trust, well, who's to say it isn't worth it?

The only thing is, you should never have asked me to hear your confession.

The Marchesa enters. The Cardinal sits, and the Marchesa kneels at the prie-dieu beside him.

MARCHESA: Bless me, Father, for I have sinned. I accuse myself of feelings of anger and doubt concerning our religion and our Holy Father the Pope.

CARDINAL: Go on.

MARCHESA: Yesterday, in public, talking about the Bishop of Fano, I said that the Holy Catholic church had become a den of perverts.

CARDINAL: Go on.

MARCHESA: I have listened to propositions that were contrary to my marriage vows.

CARDINAL: Who made these propositions to you?

MARCHESA: They were contained in a letter I read.

CARDINAL: Who wrote you the letter?

MARCHESA: I accuse myself of my own sins, not the sins of others.

CARDINAL: My daughter, you must answer me, if you expect me to grant you absolution. First of all, tell me if you answered the letter?

MARCHESA: I answered it in conversation, I did not write a reply.

CARDINAL: What did you say?

MARCHESA: I told the person who wrote me that he could come to see me, as he asked to do.

CARDINAL: And what happened when you saw him?

MARCHESA: I have already accused myself of listening to propositions that were contrary to my honor.

CARDINAL: What did you say to those propositions?

MARCHESA: What any self-respecting woman would.

CARDINAL: Did you give him any indication that those propositions might be agreeable to you?

MARCHESA: No, Father.

CARDINAL: Did you tell the person in question that you were resolved not to entertain any such propositions in the future?

MARCHESA: Yes, Father.

CARDINAL: How do you feel about this person?

MARCHESA: My feelings have nothing to do with it, I hope.

CARDINAL: Have you told your husband about this?

MARCHESA: No, Father. No self-respecting wife would upset her husband over a matter like this.

CARDINAL: And you are concealing nothing? Is there nothing that might have gone on between you and this person that you hesitate to mention?

MARCHESA: Nothing, Father.

CARDINAL: No long looks? No casual kisses?

MARCHESA: No, Father.

CARDINAL: Are you sure, my daughter?

MARCHESA: My dear brother-in-law, I am not in the habit of lying to God.

CARDINAL: And yet you refused to tell me the name of

this person when I asked you a moment ago. I cannot grant you absolution until I know.

MARCHESA: Why? It may be a sin to read a letter, but surely there's no sin in a signature. What does his name have to do with it?

CARDINAL: More than you think.

MARCHESA: Malaspina, you want to know too much. You can refuse me absolution if you want; I can go confess to the next priest I meet, he will give it to me. *(She rises)*

CARDINAL: Such emotion, Marchesa! Do you think I don't know it's the Duke you're talking about?

MARCHESA: The Duke! Well then, if you already know, why make me tell you?

CARDINAL: Why didn't you want to tell me? That's what amazes me.

MARCHESA: And what do you hope to do with the information? Do you mean to tell my husband, is that why? Yes, of course that's it. I see what a mistake it is to confess to a brother-in-law! As God is my witness, when I knelt down here I had forgotten we were related, but you certainly manage to remind me! I warn you, Cibo, have a care for your own salvation. You may be a Cardinal, but watch out!

CARDINAL: Come back and kneel down, Marchesa. Things are not as sinful as you seem to believe.

MARCHESA: What do you mean by that?

CARDINAL: Just that a confessor needs to know everything, in order to move things in the right direction, but a brother-in-law need not tell everything, given certain conditions.

MARCHESA: What conditions?

CARDINAL: I used the wrong word, excuse me, conditions

isn't quite what I meant. I meant only that the Duke is a powerful man, and a break with him could ruin even the richest families . . . but a vital secret in the right hands, hands that know what to do with it, could be a source of considerable profit.

MARCHESA: A source of profit? The right hands? What are you getting at? The way you put things, you priests, no one can ever tell what you mean.

CARDINAL: Come back and kneel down, Ricciarda. I haven't given you absolution yet.

MARCHESA: Keep talking; I haven't decided whether I want it or not.

CARDINAL *(He rises)*: Be careful, Marchesa! If you intend to work against me, you'd better look to your defenses! I make no threats—but from now on get yourself another confessor! *(He leaves)*

MARCHESA: This is incredible. He was furious! He was about to hit me! What did he mean, talking about the right hands, about moving things in the right direction? I thought he wanted to know my secret so he could tell my husband—I still think so—but if that isn't it, what does he want me to do? Become the Duke's mistress? I don't understand; Cibo wouldn't stoop to pimping for the Duke. I know him too well; he couldn't. That's work for Lorenzaccio, not him! There must be something deeper, more involved. How terrifying men can be! Ten years of smiling good manners, and suddenly this!

And what should I do now? Do I love Alessandro? No. I'm sure I don't. I said I didn't when I made my confession, and I told the truth. Oh, why did my husband have to go away just now? Why is the Duke so insistent? Why did I tell him I didn't want to see him anymore? And why, oh why, does this whole affair seem so attractive, why does it excite me so? *(She goes to the window)* Oh, Florence! What a beautiful city, and what a sorrowful place! Florence, what role do you play in all this? Who is it I really love? Is it you? Is it him?

The sound of horses, shouts below. Enter Agnolo.

AGNOLO: Signora, the Duke is here. He's just ridden into the courtyard.

MARCHESA: What a state that Malaspina has left me in. I'm beginning to shake. How strange.

SCENE TEN

The Soderini palace. Maria Soderini, Caterina, Lorenzo stretched out on the floor.

CATERINA *(Opening a book)*: Which story would you like to hear, dear?

MARIA: Cattina, you're making fun of me. You know I don't understand any of your books. They're all in Latin.

CATERINA: This one has been translated. It's a collection of stories from Roman history.

LORENZO: Oh, Roman history. I know all about Roman history. Once upon a time there was a young man named Tarquin. Tarquin the Younger.

CATERINA: Ugh! That's a murder story.

LORENZO: No, you're wrong, it's a fairy tale. The old husband was an idiot obsessed with his wife, and Tarquin was a wise and noble Duke, who gets up in

the middle of the night and goes to see if all the
pretty little girlies are safe asleep in their beds.

CATERINA: What about Lucretia? Haven't you anything
good to say about Lucretia?

LORENZO: I'm sure she enjoyed herself. She had the
pleasure of the sin, and after it was all over she had
the glory of the story. She just lay there quivering,
and when it was all over she took her little penknife
and stuck it right in her little tit.

MARIA: I know you dislike women, but why must you
insult them in front of your mother and your cousin?

LORENZO: I respect you. And I respect her. But the rest
of the world makes me sick to my stomach. Anyway,
it's a stupid story. Read me the one about Brutus.
The Brutus who took out his sword and stabbed
Caesar.

A knock at the door. Enter Bindo and Venturi.

CATERINA: It's Uncle Bindo and Baptista Venturi.

BINDO *(Aside, to Maria)*: I'll try one more time.

MARIA: We'll leave you alone; I pray to God you succeed!

Maria and Caterina leave.

BINDO: Now, Lorenzo. People are saying terrible things
about you; you must do something. You have to deny
them.

LORENZO: What things?

BINDO: They say that you fainted at the sight of a sword.

LORENZO: Do you believe them, Uncle?

BINDO: I have seen you practice with the sword before, in
Rome; but nothing would surprise me anymore,

considering the vile things you're involved in here.

LORENZO: Well, it's a true story. I did faint. Hello, Venturi. How's business? Taxes getting you down?

VENTURI: Sir, it is quite true that I am the owner of a silk factory, but you insult me to take that tone with me.

BINDO: Signor Venturi is aware of the plans that are being made nowadays among many families here in Florence. He is a distinguished friend of freedom, Lorenzo, and I insist that you treat him as one. The time for making jokes is over. You have often told us that your . . . close relationship with the Duke was only a trap you were setting for him. Is that true or not? Are you on our side, or aren't you? All the noble families of Florence agree that the Medicis are dictators and their administration is unjust and intolerable. The time has come to gather those who love their country and put an end to it. Will you stand up with us?

LORENZO: What have you got to say, Signor Venturi? Speak up, now's your chance, my uncle has stopped to take a breath. Let's hear it, if you love your country.

VENTURI: I agree completely. There's not a single word I could add.

LORENZO: Not a single word? Not one single inspiring word? Then you haven't been paying attention to Uncle Bindo. You hear the way he takes one single little word and spins it out into a long paragraph, like a yo-yo on a string? See? He raises his arm in this grand Republican gesture and then he lets his paragraph roll down the string and spin like a yo-yo. It's his way of getting kids interested in politics.

BINDO: You little punk! You show me a little respect! Now you answer me, or by God . . .

LORENZO: Oh, I'm with you, Uncle, I'm with you! Can't you tell from my haircut that I'm an enemy of the established order? Take a look at my clothes! Don't you worry, Uncle, I live and breathe love of country! You can smell love of country in my underpants!

A bell rings at the gate. The sound of horses and shouting in the courtyard below. They go to the window to look.

BINDO: My God, it's the Duke! What does he want here?

LORENZO: Me, most likely.

Enter Alessandro, followed by his guards.

What an extraordinary honor, Highness! Imagine taking the trouble to come visit your humble slave in person!

THE DUKE: Who are these people? Get rid of them, I have to talk to you alone.

LORENZO: Allow me to present my uncle, Bindo Altoviti. And this other gentleman—this other distinguished gentleman is Baptista Venturi, who manufactures silk, I'm afraid, but who does not sell it. Now, Uncle, be calm, and you too, Signor Venturi, don't get nervous because such an important man has just dropped in like this. The fact is, you're now about to get what you asked for, otherwise I'll be embarrassed to death because I thought I had some influence over His Highness and if he doesn't give you what you want that will prove I don't.

THE DUKE: What do you want, Bindo?

BINDO: Your Highness, you must excuse my nephew ...

LORENZO: The fact is, Highness, that at the moment you

don't have an ambassador to Rome. The job is open, and my uncle seems to feel that he'd be the perfect man for the job. There's not a man in Florence who loves the Medicis as much as Uncle Bindo.

THE DUKE: Is that true? Well, Bindo, I'm delighted to hear it. Come see me at the palace tomorrow.

BINDO: Your Highness, believe me, I don't know what to say . . .

LORENZO: And Signor Venturi, even though he does not sell silk, has a favor to ask of Your Highness.

THE DUKE: What favor is that?

LORENZO: The favor of putting your coat of arms up over his door, with a little sign, "By Appointment, Silk Manufacturer to the Duke of Florence." Isn't that right, Signor Venturi? Be generous, Highness, let him have it.

THE DUKE: He has it. Good. Now are we done? If you gentlemen don't mind . . .

VENTURI: Your Highness! I'm . . . I'm very grateful, I don't know how . . .

THE DUKE (To his guards): Let these two men out.

LORENZO: Have a good evening, gentlemen!

They leave.

THE DUKE: Baby, I've just made it with the Marchesa Cibo!

LORENZO: That's too bad.

THE DUKE: Why?

LORENZO: Because some of your other fucks aren't going to like it!

THE DUKE: Don't worry, she bores me already. Anyway, lover, what I want to know is the name of the woman

I saw on the way in here. She was arranging flowers at a window. Beautiful! And I've seen her before.

LORENZO: What woman? Where?

THE DUKE *(He looks out the window)*: There, in the wing opposite.

LORENZO: That's nobody.

THE DUKE: What do you mean, nobody? A body like that, you call her nobody? Goddam, that's my lady Venus!

LORENZO: She's just a neighbor.

THE DUKE: Well, goddam it, introduce me to your neighbor! Wait a minute, I know who she is. That's Caterina Ginori.

LORENZO: No.

THE DUKE: It is too, I recognize her now. It's your cousin. Goddam, I forgot how good-looking she was! Invite her to dinner some night.

LORENZO: She won't come. She's honest. She's pure.

THE DUKE: So what? A little purity might do us some good, don't you think so?

LORENZO: Well, I can ask her, if that's what you want. I warn you, though, she's a bore. She speaks Latin.

THE DUKE: So what? She doesn't fuck in Latin, does she? Come on down the hall, we can see her better from the other end.

LORENZO: Not now, lover. I haven't got the time; I'm late. I'm on my way to see the Strozzis.

THE DUKE: Christ! That old fart! What do you have to see him for?

LORENZO: Yes, that old fart. He has a problem: he can't help passing out money to the people you exile. So my plan this evening is to go eat his dinner and assure him of my undying loyalty. And later I'll have a few things to report, and tomorrow morning you can send some of your men to wake up a few people earlier than they planned.

THE DUKE: I'm lucky to have you, lover! But I swear to God I don't know why they let you in.

LORENZO: You don't know how easy it is to make an honest man believe you. That's because you've never even tried. By the way: didn't you say you wanted to have your portrait painted, as a present for someone? I've got just the man who can do it. A new little number I picked up.

THE DUKE: Good; you arrange it. But don't forget to invite your cousin. She's the reason I came to see you. Goddam, I can't get her out of my mind!

LORENZO: What about the Marchesa Cibo?

THE DUKE: I told you, she bores me. And I'm interested in your cousin!

They leave.

SCENE ELEVEN

A room in the Strozzi palace. Filippo, the Prior, Luisa, who is busy sewing, and Lorenzo stretched out on a couch.

FILIPPO: I pray to God nothing comes of this. A chance remark, and out come the knives. Someone makes an insult, he gets killed; someone kills, and he gets killed. Then the families feud. Hate takes root, children are rocked to sleep in their ancestors' coffins, and whole generations enter the world with daggers drawn.

THE PRIOR: It was my fault; I should never have told you.

But how are we supposed to put up with people like
Salviati?

FILIPPO: Oh, Leo, Leo, what difference would it make,
for Luisa or for any of us, if you hadn't told the boys?
Can't a Strozzi's honor stand against a Salviati's
word? Does a man in a palace pay attention to the
graffiti they scribble on his walls? Now it's all out of
control; Piero is in a rage at what you told him. If he
meets Salviati there will be bloodshed—my blood,
shed in the streets of Florence. Why did God make
me a father?

THE PRIOR: If someone had told me about it I wouldn't
have paid attention, but this was right to my face, and
it was so filthy I thought the bastard didn't know who
he was talking to. But he knew, all right.

FILIPPO: Oh, they know, God damn them all. They know
exactly where to strike! My little Luisa! The thought
makes my hands shake. How can I listen to reason?
God help me, is this what reason sounds like? A
shaky old man?

THE PRIOR: Piero is too full of violence. The worst thing
would be if he runs into Salviati tonight. Tomorrow
we'll all be able to look at things more calmly.

FILIPPO: Don't delude yourself. Piero will kill him, or get
himself killed. *(He opens the window)* Where are they
now? It's night. I hate these black streets. There's
blood on them somewhere, I know it.

THE PRIOR: Get hold of yourself, close that window.

FILIPPO: I am the head of this family, and I suffer
because of it. Florence! My noble blood flows in the
veins of forty of your sons! It stains your streets! But
have pity on old Strozzi tonight, he is afraid for his

boy. Take care of his family, the day may come when you will need it!

LUISA: Father, please! You're making me afraid!

FILIPPO: See how the fathers of this city must wait for their children! My poor country! A drunken remark and we explode with anger, all our friends and children rush into the street—but the injuries done to the body politic cannot call out a single weapon. Tyranny had to slap me in the face before I could say "It's time to act!"

Enter Piero and Tommaso.

PIERO: It's done. Salviati is dead. *(He kisses his sister)*

LUISA: How horrible! You're all covered with blood.

PIERO: We waited for him at the Arch Street corner. Francesco stopped his horse, Tommaso got him in the leg, and I . . .

LUISA: Stop it! I don't want to hear!

LORENZO *(He gets up)*: You look beautiful, Piero, you look like a god of vengeance.

PIERO: Who's that? Lorenzaccio! What are you doing here? *(He turns to his father)* When will you stop letting him into the house? Don't you realize what he is? Didn't they tell you he wouldn't fight with Sior Maurizio?

FILIPPO: I know all that already. If Lorenzo is here, it means I have good reasons for wanting him here. We'll discuss it another time.

PIERO: Good reasons for letting that scum in the house! One of these days I'll find a good reason for heaving him through a window. I don't care what you say, it

makes me want to throw up, seeing that faggot lying
all over our furniture!

FILIPPO: That's enough! You talk like a fool! I hope to
God what you've done tonight doesn't turn out to be
a disaster for all of us. You'll have to find a place to
hide.

PIERO: Me, hide? Why should I hide, for godsakes? It was
a public insult: he insulted us in the middle of the
street, I killed him in the middle of the street, and
tomorrow I intend to go out in the middle of the
street and tell everyone I meet exactly what I did.
Why should I hide? I avenged our honor!

FILIPPO: Oh, my son. Come with me, we have to talk.

They leave.

SCENE TWELVE

The Duke's bedroom. Clothes strewn on the bed. The Duke, naked to the waist, poses for Tebaldeo, who is painting his portrait. Giomo plays the guitar and sings.

GIOMO:

> See the pretty naked ladies
> by the waterside,
> come and hang out by the water,
> watch those ladies slip and slide . . .

LORENZO *(He enters, and sprawls on the bed)*: How is it
going? Are you pleased with my little friend? *(He picks
up the Duke's chain-mail coat)* You have a fabulous
chain mail, lover. But it must make you sweat.

THE DUKE: If it did I wouldn't wear it. That's steel thread; the sharpest knife couldn't cut it. Anyway it's light as silk. There's not another one like it in the whole world. I almost never take it off. I never take it off, in fact.

LORENZO: You're right, it's always under your jacket, isn't it? I remember the other day when we were out together, I rode double with you, with my arms around you, tight, and I could feel it. It's a smart idea. *(He hides the chain mail in his jacket)*

THE DUKE: It's not that I don't trust people—it's just habit, like you say. I got used to wearing it when I was in the army.

LORENZO: I love your clothes! And your gloves. There's always an odor on your gloves. Why are you posing half naked? You should be wearing your chain mail. It would look spectacular.

THE DUKE: It was the painter's idea. He says the best portraits are always half naked. Look at all those Greek and Roman statues.

LORENZO: Giomo wants to try *that* song, he needs a backup. Where the hell is my guitar? *(He leaves)*

THE DUKE: I knew there was something I wanted to ask you. Listen, you dumb hunk. Who was that boy you were working over yesterday? You were getting off on it, I could tell.

GIOMO: Oh, that was just the boy next door.

THE DUKE: What happened to him?

GIOMO: I think this morning they were arranging his funeral.

THE DUKE *(He laughs)*: When my Giomo hits, he hits hard.

GIOMO: That's easy for you to say. There's lots of times

I've seen you kill a man with one slash.

THE DUKE: I did? I must have been drunk. When I'm
feeling good, even my looks can kill. *(To Tebaldeo)*
What's the matter, baby? Why is your hand shaking?

TEBALDEO: Nothing, Your Highness. It's. . . . I think
that's about all I can do today.

GIOMO *(He looks out the window)*: What the hell is
Lorenzo doing? He's leaning way over the well in the
middle of the courtyard. Is that where he keeps his
guitar?

THE DUKE: Giomo, give me my clothes. Where's my
chain mail?

GIOMO: I can't find it. It was here just a while ago, what
happened to it?

THE DUKE: Lorenzino was playing with it; he must have
thrown it in a corner somewhere, he's such an
enviable slob.

GIOMO: I don't believe this. I saw that chain mail just five
minutes ago. It's gone!

THE DUKE: You must be kidding. It's got to be here.

GIOMO: Look for yourself, Highness! It's not that big a
room!

THE DUKE: Renzo was playing with it right there, on the
bed.

Enter Lorenzo with a guitar.

What did you do with my chain mail? We can't find it
anywhere.

LORENZO: I put it back where I found it. Wait a minute.
No, I must have dumped it on this chair. No, it was
on the bed, I guess. I don't remember. Anyway, I

found my guitar. *(He starts to play and sing)* "See the
pretty naked ladies . . . "

GIOMO: Where was it, in the well in the courtyard? I saw
you looking down there. What's the matter, do holes
in the ground turn you on?

LORENZO: I like to spit in the water and watch the
ripples. I like that more than anything in the world.
After drinking and fucking, it's my favorite sport. *(He
plays and sings)* " . . . want to lie down by the water,
teach those ladies how to ride . . . "

THE DUKE: I don't believe this! What the fuck happened
to my chain mail? This is only about the second time
in my life I've ever taken it off, except when I go to
bed.

LORENZO: Oh forget it, for Chrissake! You're the son of
a pope, not a houseboy. The servants can look for it.

THE DUKE: Fuck you. You took it.

LORENZO: If I was the Duke of Florence, I'd be worried
about more than my chain mail. Oh, I forgot—I
talked to my pretty cousin. Everything's easy. Come
here a minute, lover, I'll tell you what she said.

He takes the Duke aside.

GIOMO: Spitting in the well. That's crazy. I want to find
that chain mail, just to get rid of a little idea I keep
having. Fucking Lorenzaccio! It's got to be here
someplace.

A commotion in the courtyard. Salviati shouts up from below.

SALVIATI: Alessandro Medici! Open your window and

see what they've done to one of your friends!

THE DUKE *(He goes to the window)*: Who's making all that noise down there? Salviati! Is that you? You're all covered with mud. What happened?

SALVIATI: It's the Strozzis! They killed me, I'm dying!

THE DUKE: Which Strozzi was it? And what did they do it for?

SALVIATI: Because I said their sister was in love with you, Duke. The Strozzi thought it was an insult, and a bunch of them jumped me. Piero and Tommaso. . . . I don't know who about the rest.

THE DUKE: Get him up here. And get the Strozzi! Get them into prison tonight! I want them hanged in the morning!

SCENE THIRTEEN

Lorenzo's bedroom. Lorenzo and Scoronconcolo wrestling.

SCORONCONCOLO: Master, haven't you had enough?

LORENZO: No, go ahead, shout louder! Take that! Take that! Die, you scum! Die! Die!

SCORONCONCOLO: Help! Murder! Help! He's trying to cut my throat!

LORENZO: Die! Die! Die! Hit the floor, go on!

SCORONCONCOLO: Help, guards! Help! He's killing me! That bastard Lorenzo is killing me!

LORENZO: Die, scum! Bleed, pig, when I stick you! Right in the heart! Right in the gut! Bleed! Now hit him! Now kill him! Shout! Hack him open, pull out his guts! I want to cut him up in little pieces and eat him, eat him, eat him! I want my teeth in his throat! I want both my arms in him up to the elbows! *(He falls across Scoronconcolo, exhausted)*

SCORONCONCOLO *(He wipes his forehead)*: You have a weird game going, Master, a very weird game. And you play it like an animal. Jesus. You really get into this shit, you sound like a cage full of lions and tigers, you know?

LORENZO: I want blood for my wedding day! Look at the sun! It's dry, it's dead, it needs a drink, it wants blood! And I'll give it blood! I'll give it *his* blood! I want my revenge!

SCORONCONCOLO *(He is concerned)*: You're crazy. You're sick.

LORENZO: Coward . . . coward . . . scummy punk . . . look at the skinny little boy . . . think of all the fathers, all their daughters . . . and all the goodbyes! Goodbye, goodbye, goodbye forever. . . . Even the kids write goodbye in graffiti. . . . Oh, the skull! the skull!

SCORONCONCOLO: Master, there's somebody you don't like. *(He splashes water in his face)* Come on, Master, come on, it's not worth the energy, throwing yourself all around like this. Look. You have feelings. We all have feelings. Some people have cleaner feelings than others. You taught me a lot about that; if it weren't for you I'd still be on the streets. Look, Master, if you have an enemy, just tell me. I can get rid of him, very easy, and no one will ever know.

LORENZO: Nothing's the matter. I told you I just like to scare the neighbors.

SCORONCONCOLO: Well, they must be used to it by now, ever since we started playing these games up in

your room. You could cut thirty guys to pieces and
nobody would pay any attention. Nobody even opens
a window and yells "shut up" anymore.

LORENZO *(He sits up)*: You're right. They don't.

SCORONCONCOLO: I know you have an enemy, Master.
Now you listen to me, there's nothing worse than
hating someone. Bad for your stomach. You got two
guys out in the sunshine, one of them is always going
to hate the other one's shadow, right? But I got the
medicine right here. You want me to cure you? *(He
holds out his sword)*

LORENZO: Did that medicine ever cure you?

SCORONCONCOLO: Four times. No, five. I remember
this one time in Padua . . .

LORENZO: Let me see that. God, what a fabulous blade.

SCORONCONCOLO: Try it, you'll see.

LORENZO: You're a good doctor, you know exactly what's
the matter with me. You're right, I have an enemy.
But to kill him I need a sword that has never killed
anyone else in the world. The sword that kills him
has his name on it.

SCORONCONCOLO: What is his name?

LORENZO: What's it to you? *(Pause)* Are you my faithful
slave?

SCORONCONCOLO: I'd do anything for you. For you, I'd
crucify Christ all over again.

LORENZO: Then I'll tell you my plan. I am going to kill
him right here, in my bedroom. That's why I carry on
like this up here, so the neighbors won't suspect.
Now listen to me, and get this straight. If I get him
with the first blow, I warn you, don't touch him. But
I'm a sissy, remember? And he's a wild animal. So if

he fights back, then I'm counting on you to hold him, just his hands, that's all, understand? He's mine. He belongs to me. I'll let you know when.

SCORONCONCOLO: Amen.

SCENE FOURTEEN

The Strozzi palace. Enter Filippo and Piero.

PIERO: I missed the sonofabitch! I aimed right at his heart, and I missed! That bastard rolled over and played dead, and I never finished him off!

FILIPPO *(Wearily)*: What difference does it make? If he's still alive, it's an even better revenge. They say he'll be a cripple for the rest of his life.

PIERO: Father—you are a great patriot, and are an even better father. But this is something you don't want to be involved in. Just stay out of this, from now on.

FILIPPO: Now what are you going to do? Can't you spend fifteen minutes without thinking of violence?

PIERO: No, goddam it! I can't live another fifteen minutes in the polluted air of this city! The sky over my head is as dark as a dungeon, the streets are full of faggots and drunks, night and day they stink with piss and vomit!

FILIPPO: Where are you going?

PIERO: Why do you want to know? *(Pause)* I'm going to the Pazzis.

FILIPPO: Wait, I'll go with you.

PIERO: Not tonight, Father. We don't want you there tonight.

FILIPPO: Why? What is going on? Tell me honestly.

PIERO: It's our business. There are about fifty of us, the Rucellai and a lot of others, and we have had it up to here with that bastard!

FILIPPO: So?

PIERO: So sometimes all it takes to start an avalanche is a pebble no bigger than that.

FILIPPO: Have you made plans? Have you taken precautions? Set up security? Oh, you are children, children! You think life and death is only a game! You think all it takes is a little sword practice and a few drinks, and you're off, as if it were a masquerade party or a football game! What do you know about a republic, about workingmen in factories, about farmers in their fields, citizens in the streets, the life of an entire nation? Good God of justice, what can you know about the happiness of mankind? These are things God himself dares not touch, he leaves them to man to accomplish!

PIERO: The Medicis are a disease, and there's no medicine against them! But a good sharp scalpel, that will cure any disease. A man who gets bitten by a poison snake can't just wait for the doctor, he has to cut the wound!

FILIPPO: And when you have overthrown the present system, what will you put in its place?

PIERO: We intend to get rid of the murderers who rule Florence! At least we can't get anything worse!

FILIPPO: And you've made up your minds? There'll be no turning back?

PIERO: Let me go, Father. I have to do this alone.

FILIPPO: Oh my son! I see now that you are serious, that you do intend to act. Take me with you, I can help.

Don't leave without me, son. I won't make any long speeches, I promise you.

PIERO: Yes, Father, come join us! You are the true leader of us all, come see the dream of your lifetime fulfilled! Liberty is ripe, now is the time to pluck it from the tree! Come join us, you are the old gardener of Florence, come see how the tree you watered has grown!

They leave.

SCENE FIFTEEN

A street. A German officer and some soldiers enter, with Tommaso Strozzi as their prisoner.

THE OFFICER: If he's not at home, we'll find him with the Pazzis.

TOMMASO: Just go where you're supposed to, never mind him. You'll pay for this later!

THE OFFICER: Don't try to push me around. I'm following the Duke's orders, and I don't answer to anybody else.

TOMMASO: Asshole! You arrest a Strozzi because a Medici tells you to?

A group of citizens forms around them.

FIRST CITIZEN: Why are you arresting this young man? This is Filippo Strozzi's son.

SECOND CITIZEN: Let him go, we'll take responsibility for him.

FIRST CITIZEN: Yes, we'll take responsibility for the
     Strozzi. You turn him loose, or you're the ones who'll
     be in trouble!
THE OFFICER: Break it up, break it up! Get back to your
     houses, you scum, and let the Duke's guards through!

Enter Piero and Filippo.

PIERO: What is all this? What's going on? Tommaso, what
     happened?
A CITIZEN: Stop them, Filippo, they're taking your son to
     prison.
FILIPPO: To prison? On whose orders?
PIERO: To prison? Do you know who you're dealing with?
THE OFFICER: Arrest that man!

The soldiers arrest Piero.

PIERO: Let me go, you bastards, or I'll slit your guts!
FILIPPO: Officer, who ordered these arrests?
THE OFFICER *(He shows him the Duke's warrant)*: Here's
     the warrant. I have orders to arrest Piero and
     Tommaso Strozzi.

The soldiers begin to disperse the crowd, which throws stones.

PIERO: What are we accused of? What did we do? Help
     us, you people, let's teach this scum a lesson! *(He
     draws his sword)*
THE OFFICER: Over here, give us a hand with him.

The soldiers surround Piero and disarm him.

All right, let's go! March! And a butt in the backside for the first one of you who comes too close! We'll teach you to mind your own business!

PIERO: You can't arrest me without a warrant from the Council of Eight. I don't give a damn for Alessandro's orders! Where's the warrant from the Eight?

THE OFFICER: That's exactly where we're taking you. To the Council of Eight.

PIERO: But what's the charge against me?

A VOICE IN THE CROWD: What's the matter, Filippo, why are you letting them take your boys to the Council?

PIERO: Answer me, I want to know what's the charge against me!

THE OFFICER: That's none of my business.

The soldiers go off with Piero and Tommaso, the crowd follows them.

PIERO *(As he goes off)*: Don't worry, Father, I'll be back in time for supper. And the bastard will have to pay for this!

FILIPPO: *(Alone, he sits down on a bench)*: All my children. I won't have them long, things go so fast. Oh, Christ! To think that justice pimps for that man! The honor of the Strozzi family insulted in public, and the courts obey the orders of a drunken punk. God in heaven! Only an hour ago I spoke out against rebellion and revolt, and now look at what they make me swallow! The time has come to act!

Enter Lorenzo.

LORENZO: Have you taken up begging at street corners,
     Filippo?
FILIPPO: I am a beggar for justice! And my honor is in
     rags!
LORENZO: Father, what's wrong? Why are you crying?
FILIPPO: We must get rid of the Medicis, Lorenzo. You
     must help me! You are a Medici in name only. It's
     time for a man to step out from behind the mask you
     wear! If you have ever been an honorable man, be
     one today. Piero and Tommaso are in prison.
LORENZO: Yes, I know.
FILIPPO: You know? Is that all you can say?
LORENZO: What do you want me to say? Tell me, and I'll
     give you an answer.
FILIPPO: Say? Say? Act! It's time to act! Oh, Lorenzo, the
     time has come. Lorenzo, they curse you, they call you
     names, and in spite of everything I have always
     welcomed you, I have opened my house and my heart
     to you, now, speak to me now. Didn't you tell me
     about the other Lorenzo, a different man hidden
     behind the Lorenzo we all see? A man who loves his
     country and his friends? You did, and I believed you.
     Tell me I wasn't wrong!
LORENZO: I am the man you want, Filippo. I swear by
     the sun in heaven, I am the man.
FILIPPO: Oh, my friend, you must not make fun of a
     desperate old man. If you are speaking the truth, then
     act! Act! You have been playing a role, a pervert, a
     gutter-monster, but I always believed in you, I treated
     you honestly. Now be honest with me. Act! You must,
     I can't. You are young, I am old.
LORENZO: Piero and Tommaso are in prison; is that all?
FILIPPO: Oh God in heaven, is that all? Yes, all, all—it's

not much, is it, two of my children taken off like common thieves, to be strung up tomorrow at the gate of the Citadel. That's nothing, is it?

LORENZO: You don't have to use that tone with me. My own sadness is so dark the midnight sky is a blinding light beside it. *(He sits down next to Filippo)*

FILIPPO: How can I let my children die? Oh, I know so well how it all works! The Council of Eight! A bench of marble men, a graveyard row, and it all ends in a word, a single word from which there is no appeal! A single word, you understand? Oh, let them kill what they want, whenever, however, but not my boys, not my boys!

LORENZO: Piero is a man. He will stand and defend himself, and they will let him go.

FILIPPO: Oh, Piero, my boy, my oldest! And all this because of one remark by a Salviati!

LORENZO: You don't understand. Salviati was trying to seduce your daughter for Alessandro. Our Duke claims his ducal rights even with pimps.

FILIPPO: And we do nothing! We do not act! Oh, Lorenzo, Lorenzo! You're a young man, speak to me, I'm weak, my feelings are too much involved in all this. Can't you see I'm worn out, tell me what you think, I'll do what you say.

LORENZO: My good old friend, do nothing. Go home.

FILIPPO: No, I'll go to the Pazzis. There are fifty young men there, all sworn to act. I'll speak to them, they'll listen. Tonight I'll invite the forty members of my family to dinner, I'll explain to them what's happened. We will do something, you'll see.

LORENZO: Filippo, the devil has more than one face. Be careful. He is tempting you.

FILIPPO: What do you mean?

LORENZO: There are temptations more attractive than angels. Liberty, patriotism, the good of humanity—words like that are the silver scales of the Tempter's flaming wings. Be careful!

FILIPPO: I can barely understand what you're saying.

LORENZO: Is that really all you want to do—get your sons out of jail? There's something else, isn't there, another idea, something powerful and grand that moves you like a war-engine, off to meet those young men. Isn't there?

FILIPPO: Yes! There is! I want the injustice done to my family to be the signal for liberty! For me, and for us all. That's why I'm going.

LORENZO: Be careful, Filippo. You are about to act for the good of humanity.

FILIPPO: What is that supposed to mean? Are you really cynical through and through? You used to talk to me about the precious contents of your soul—is that what you've been hiding?

LORENZO: I am precious for you, that's true, because I intend to kill Alessandro.

FILIPPO: You?

LORENZO: Me. Tomorrow, or the day after, Alessandro Medici will vanish from Florence, the way the sun disappears at night.

FILIPPO: But. . . . But your action will bring us liberty—if in fact you do it. Why is it wrong for me to think about liberty?

LORENZO: Filippo, be careful, be careful. You have lived sixty honorable years. That's too dear a sum to gamble on a throw of the dice.

FILIPPO: If that cryptic remark is supposed to mean

something, let me know what, will you? You are
beginning to make me very angry.

LORENZO: Filippo, no matter what you see in me now, I
was once an honest man. I believed in goodness and
human dignity. I wept tears over the fate of Italy. *(He
pauses)* I was innocent, pure as gold. For twenty years
I kept my thoughts to myself, and an enormous
charge of energy must have been building up inside
me, because suddenly, one night, I was sitting in the
ruins of the Coliseum, I stood up—I don't know
why—and I raised my arms to heaven and I swore
that I would kill one of the tyrants who ruled my
country. I don't know where that strange idea came
from. I used to wonder if that was what people felt
when they fell in love.

FILIPPO: I have always believed whatever you told me, but
this—

LORENZO: I know, I think sometimes it was all a dream. I
used to be happy, you know. I was calm, my hands
didn't shake; I was a good person, but, to my
everlasting unhappiness, I wanted to be great. I have
to admit it: if God hadn't given me the resolution to
kill a tyrant, no matter who, my pride would have
done it. All the Caesars of this world made me think
only of Brutus.

FILIPPO: But pride in virtue is a noble kind of pride. Why
should you feel strange about it?

LORENZO: You'll never be able to understand what it was
like, that idea. Not unless you go crazy too. It began
to grow inside me. You would have to take a scalpel
and cut open my guts in order to understand the
fever, the fire I felt—and that fire forged the Lorenzo
you see in front of you now.

FILIPPO: You constantly astonish me.

LORENZO: At first I wanted to kill the Pope. Clement the Seventh. But they banished me from Rome before I could do it. And so I began my project all over again with his son, with Alessandro. You see, I wanted to act alone, without anyone's help. I didn't want to make speeches, play politics, start a popular uprising—what I wanted was to meet Alessandro face to face, to fight tyranny as it lived and breathed in *him* and kill it *there*, then to carry my bloody sword before the body politic and push it under the speechmakers' noses.

FILIPPO: You wear a mask of iron, Lorenzo.

LORENZO: Alessandro lived a life of complete obscenity. I had to make my cousin like me, so I had to sink down to his level, join him in his filth, in the sewer full of wine and blood he had made of Florence. I had to gain his confidence, so I became his lover and his pimp, I kissed him when his mouth still stank of rape. And I was innocent then. But I didn't hesitate. I did what I had to. And what I've become as a result, what people call me—never mind. But I want you to know I suffered. There are some wounds that never heal. I don't care, though. That's not what all this is about.

FILIPPO: Then why turn your head away? Why are you crying?

LORENZO: I'm not crying. My face is a plaster cast, it doesn't show any feelings at all. In a little while Alessandro will enter a room he will never leave alive. An entire army couldn't penetrate his guards and defenses, but his body will soon be naked beneath my hands, and all I will have to do is push my weapon into his heart. Then it will all be over.

FILIPPO: You are the new Brutus—our Brutus—if all this is true.

LORENZO: Oh Filippo, poor Filippo. I used to think I was Brutus. But now I know what people are really like. And I warn you, don't get involved.

FILIPPO: Why?

LORENZO: Because you've been living alone too long, Filippo. You're like a lighthouse shining beside the sea of humanity, motionless: all you can see is your own reflection in the water. You're alone, so you think it's a vast magnificent panorama. You haven't sounded the depths. You simply believe in the beauty of God's creation. But I have spent all this time in the water, diving deep into the howling ocean of life, deeper than anyone. While you were admiring the surface, I saw the shipwrecks, the drowned bodies, the monsters of the deep.

FILIPPO: Your sadness breaks my heart.

LORENZO: I'm telling you all this because I see you now the way I was then, and on the point of doing what I did then. You and I have read too many history books. I don't hate human beings; it's just that the history books are wrong because they show us human beings different from the way they really are. Do you want my advice, Filippo? Do you want to save your sons? Then do nothing. That's the best way to get them back after a little scolding. If you want to do something for the good of humanity, then I suggest you cut your hands off, because you'll soon discover you're the only one willing to use them.

FILIPPO: Poor boy. I can see how the role you've had to play could give you such ideas. You chose a worthy goal, but you have had to follow an unworthy path to reach it, and now you think all the rest of the world is like the part of it you've experienced.

LORENZO: No, it's just that for a long time I was dreaming, and now I'm awake. I have seen life, and it's a rotten mess, believe me. If you hold anything sacred, don't get involved.

FILIPPO: Stop this! Why do you want to take away the only crutch I have left in my old age? I still believe in all the things you say are only dreams. I believe in goodness, in purity, in liberty.

LORENZO: Look at me, Filippo. Me, Lorenzaccio. Why don't the kids in the street throw rocks at me when I pass by? There are young girls' beds in this town still soaked with my sweat—why don't their fathers knife me when they see me? Oh, Filippo, it's worse: when I stop at the door of some poor family's house, the mother herself shows me her beautiful young sons and daughters, and smiles at me with a smile that would make Judas sick—and I smile back and I grope them and jingle the money in my pockets and I get sick with rage!

FILIPPO: Why tempt them if it makes you feel that way?

LORENZO: Am *I* the tempter? God! I can still remember the first girl I seduced for him: I wanted to cry, but she only laughed! At me! Oh, Filippo! That's when I realized that everyone I met was doing exactly the same thing I was: they all wore masks—and they lowered them when they saw me coming. Human beings recognized me, they knew I was one of them, and they dropped their pants and raised their skirts to show me that we belonged together. I saw men the way they really are, and I said to myself: who am I doing this for? I watched the faces I saw around me, I kept asking myself: that one: when I have done this act, will he act differently? Will he become a better person? I kept watching and watching, the way a lover watches his fiancée while he waits for the wedding!

FILIPPO: If all you saw was evil, then I feel sorry for you, but I can't believe you. Of course evil exists, but not without the good, just as shadows exist, but not without light.

LORENZO: I know perfectly well there are good men in the world—but what good are they? What power do they have? There is no way they can act! All I can see ahead for me is that my life will be over and it will have meant nothing to anyone, just as what I say now means nothing to you.

FILIPPO: Poor child. But if you are honest, then once you have freed your country you will be honest again.

LORENZO: Filippo, Filippo, I was honest once upon a time. But when you have lifted the veil of truth you cannot let it go; you stand there staring at the face of humanity until death comes and closes your eyes.

FILIPPO: No sickness lasts forever; vice is a sickness, and even it can be cured.

LORENZO: It's too late for that. I've learned my dirty job too well. I put on vice like a masquerade costume, and now it sticks to my skin. I really am scum.

FILIPPO: You have chosen a dangerous path, I agree; but why shouldn't there be a better path that takes me to the same place? What I intend to do is appeal to the people, and to act out in the open.

LORENZO: Be careful, Filippo. Believe me, you will always have human nature to deal with.

FILIPPO: I believe in the honesty of men who believe in the Republic.

LORENZO: I'll make a bet with you. I intend to kill
    Alessandro. Once I've accomplished that, it should be
    easy for the men who believe in the Republic to set
    up a republic, the most beautiful republic the world
    has ever known. If they have the people on their side,
    that's all they need. And I'll bet you that neither they
    nor the people will do a thing. All I want you to do is
    stay out of it.

FILIPPO: But why bother to kill the Duke, if that's what
    you think?

LORENZO: You ask me that to my face? Look at me. Once
    I was good, and innocent, and beautiful.

FILIPPO: What a bottomless pit you show me!

LORENZO: You ask me why I am going to kill Alessandro?
    What should I do, kill myself? Jump in the Arno?
    Don't you understand that this murder is the only
    honorable thing I have left? Don't you understand that
    for two years I have been slipping slowly down a
    vertical rockface, and that this murder is the only
    blade of grass I've been able to hold onto? Do you
    think because I've lost all shame that I've lost all my
    pride as well? Oh, believe me, if I could have my
    honor back, I'd spare that stable boy—but I've gotten
    to like it, don't you understand? I love drinking and
    gambling and fucking! I love violence! I'm addicted to
    it! If there's anything in me that you can still respect,
    it's this murder. Whether men understand me or not,
    whether they act or not, *I* will have acted. All my
    self-respect sits on the point of my knife, and whether
    God turns his head or not when he hears me strike, I
    don't care. Humanity? I'll flip you for it, heads or tails,
    on Alessandro's grave. In two days, humanity will have
    to appear before the supreme court of my will!

Act Two

SCENE ONE

The Marchesa Cibo's room. She is dressing in front of her mirror: jewels and an elaborate dressing gown.

MARCHESA: Whenever I think that all this is now *a fact*, it still seems like a piece of news someone told me only a moment ago. What a dangerous rockface this life can be! It is almost nine o'clock, and here I am, dressed like this, waiting to receive the Duke! Never mind. I don't care what happens. I must find out what power I have over him.

Enter Cardinal Cibo.

CARDINAL: Marchesa! What a display! What a hothouse flower you have become!

MARCHESA: You must excuse me, Cardinal—I can't see you now—I'm expecting a friend . . .

CARDINAL: I'm going, I'm going. And that door I see half-open, and that tiny paradise beyond it, is that your bedroom? Perhaps I could wait for you there?

MARCHESA: No, not in my bedroom—anywhere else. . . . Now you must excuse me, I'm in something of a hurry . . .

CARDINAL: I shall return at a more convenient moment. *(He leaves)*

MARCHESA: Why is that priest always here? He circles me like a vulture! Every time I turn around, there he is! What is he doing, waiting for me to die so he can give me the last rites?

Enter a page, who whispers in her ear.

Good, I'll be right there. *(She gives a last look at the mirror, then leaves)*

SCENE TWO

The Soderini palace. Enter Maria and Caterina, who carries a letter.

CATERINA: Oh, my dear! Listen to this letter. *(She reads)* "I know Lorenzo has told you about me, but only I can tell you how much I love you. This letter will tell you what you will soon hear from my mouth. And it is signed with the blood from my heart. Alessandro Medici." It was just delivered. It has my name on it, otherwise I wouldn't believe my eyes. Tell me what all this means.

MARIA: He loves you! Oh, God help us, he says he loves you! Where did he see you? Have you spoken to him?

CATERINA: No, never. A messenger gave me this as I was on my way out of church this morning.

MARIA: Lorenzo has told you about me, he says. Oh, Caterina, my own son! To make his cousin the Duke's mistress, no, not even his mistress, there's another word for what he wants.

CATERINA: But I thought the Duke was in love with . . . excuse me, dear, but I thought he was in love with the Marchesa Cibo . . . at least that's what someone told me . . .

MARIA: If you can call what he does love.

CATERINA: How can he not be ashamed to write like this? Come, dear. Let's go talk to Lorenzo about this.

MARIA: Let me take your arm. I don't know what's the matter with me, I've had a fever every night now. Oh, my poor Caterina! I've gone through so much already, why did you have to show me that letter?

They leave.

SCENE THREE

The Marchesa's bedroom. The Marchesa is in bed with the Duke.

MARCHESA: That's the way my mind works. I'd love you that way.

THE DUKE: Words, words, words.

MARCHESA: You men, none of this means anything to you! A woman gives up peace of mind, honor, reputation, sometimes even her children, gives up everything for a man, she gives herself, finally, that's what they say, don't they, "she gave herself to him. . . . " And all for what? To find out men won't listen to her! All you men expect from a woman is talk about clothes and sex—clothes for her and sex for you. If she wants to talk about anything else you can't stand it.

THE DUKE: You're wide awake and still dreaming.

MARCHESA: Yes, by God, I am! I do have dreams, don't you? Or is it true that dictators never dream, because they can change their smallest fantasies into realities if they want to? Even their nightmares are carved in marble. Alessandro, Alessandro, think what power there is in the phrase: "I can if I want to." Even God can't say more than that!

THE DUKE: Let's not talk anymore about it, sweetheart, it wears me out.

MARCHESA: Do you know what it means to be a king? What a rush in the veins that must be! Imagine how that old man in the Vatican would shake if you were to spread your wings, my eagle! You could do it! The Emperor is far away, the garrison soldiers are devoted to you. And the day you win over the whole country to your side. . . . Can you imagine what it is to hold an entire nation in your arms?

THE DUKE: All I care about are the taxes. As long as they pay their taxes, I don't care who holds who in whose arms.

MARCHESA: But haven't you ever wondered what future generations will say about you? Think of your great ancestor, the Father of his Country. Declare Florence an independent nation, protest the treaty with the Emperor, draw your sword and show it to the world—its light will blind them all! You're still young, no one has made up his mind about you yet. You've had bad advisors, you've made mistakes, but there's still time to change. When people are grateful, they will pardon their rulers most anything.

THE DUKE: Sweetheart, please, please. That's enough.

MARCHESA: Well then, suppose you don't change. Suppose the day comes when the people of Florence forget the dark meteor of your administration. . . . What will they say about you when they look at the graves of their relatives surrounding your tomb? Are you sure your last resting place will be an easy one? You never pray, you never go to church, all you think about are the taxes, are you so sure Eternity ignores all that?

THE DUKE: I love your legs.

MARCHESA: Listen to me. You're thickheaded, I know, but you're not an evil person, you're not, my God, I know you're not. Just think for a moment, it won't hurt, just think about what I'm saying. Doesn't any of this make any sense to you? Do you think I'm completely crazy?

THE DUKE: Everything you say goes right over my head. What am I doing that's so bad? I'm a lot better ruler than most of my neighbors—by God, I'm one hell of a lot better than the Pope. You're just like those Strozzis, always talk, talk, talk, and you know how I hate them. You want me to revolt against the Emperor. . . . Look, sweetheart, the Emperor is my father-in-law, for godsake! You think the people of Florence don't like me; well, I happen to think they *do* like me, so there! Anyway, even if you're right and they don't, what have I got to be afraid of?

MARCHESA: You're not afraid of your own people, but you're afraid of the Emperor! Look, you have killed or exiled hundreds of citizens! Do you think you can take care of that simply by wearing a chain-mail jacket all the time?

THE DUKE: Lay off it, will you, I've had enough.

MARCHESA: Oh, you make me so angry, I say things I don't want to say. My love, you're very brave, everyone knows you're brave. You are as brave as you are beautiful. All the awful things you've done have been because you're young, because you get carried away, how should I know? Maybe it's the hot blood in your veins, maybe it's this hot sun that stifles us all. Listen to me, I don't want all this to be a waste, I don't want my name to go down on a list of public enemies just because I love you. I know, I'm a woman, and you want beautiful women, and there are women more beautiful than me, but don't you have—listen to me, damn you! Don't you have anything, anything *here*? *(She pounds with her fists at his heart)*

THE DUKE: What a devil! You calm down, darling, you calm down right now.

MARCHESA: You listen to me! All right, I'll admit it, I'm ambitious, but it's ambition for you, not for me! I'm ambitious for you! For you and for Florence because I love you both! God, why do you make me go through all this? Why do you hurt me so?

THE DUKE: You're hurt? Where?

MARCHESA: Oh, stop it, why do you always do this? Listen to me. I know I bore you, but listen to me. I tell you, the people of Florence think of you as the return of the Black Death, I tell you there isn't a room in this city where your picture isn't stuck up on the wall with a knife through the heart! There. I may

be crazy, you may hate me tomorrow, but I don't care.
At least now you know.

THE DUKE: You watch it! You make me lose my temper,
you're in for trouble!

MARCHESA: In for trouble! I *am* in trouble! I'm already in
trouble!

THE DUKE: We can talk about this some other time.
Right now I have to go. I'm supposed to go hunting.

MARCHESA: And I'm in trouble! You leave me in trouble!

THE DUKE: Why? And why give me those black looks?
What the hell do you want to get involved in politics
for anyway? For godsake, you're a woman, you're all
woman, too, and you're good at it. Why not just leave
it at that? You pray too much, that's your problem.
Help me with my clothes, I'm all unbuttoned.

MARCHESA: Goodbye, Alessandro.

The Duke kisses her. Enter the Cardinal.

CARDINAL: Ah! Pardon, Highness, I thought my sister
was alone. How awkward! And all my fault, too. I
hope you'll forgive me.

THE DUKE: Forgive you for what? Listen, Malaspina,
you're acting like a priest; priests always think people
are doing what they're not supposed to be doing.
Besides, it's none of your goddam business.

He exits with the Cardinal.

MARCHESA *(Alone, she picks up a mirror and looks at her
reflection)*: No, my dear. This isn't the role for you.
You are much too proud.

SCENE FOUR

The Strozzi palace. The forty Strozzi, about to sit down to supper.

FILIPPO: Sit down, my children. You all know your own places. You are my family. I have gathered you together to tell you my sorrow. Salviati insulted my daughter in public, in front of her brother Leo. Piero and Tommaso fought with Salviati, and Alessandro Medici has had them arrested to avenge his bully.

THE GUESTS: Death to the Medicis!

FILIPPO: I am the head of this family; how can I allow them to insult us? We are as powerful as the Medicis! So are the Ruccellai, the Aldobrandini, and twenty other noble families. What gives them the right to murder our children, and us no right to murder theirs? It must begin with us! We must raise a cry of alarm, and bring down upon Florence the army of eagles that have been exiled from the nest. Tonight you must help me free my sons; tomorrow we will go together to the gates of all the noble families of the city. Florence has eighty great palaces, and out of each one of them will come a band like ours, once Liberty knocks at the gate!

THE GUESTS: Long live Liberty!

FILIPPO: Before God I swear that only a just revenge drives me to revolt; I am a rebel because God made me a father. Neither ambition, pride, nor profit impels me. My cause is loyal, honorable, and holy. Fill your glasses and stand, all of you! Revenge is a sacrament we can share without fear, in the presence of God. I drink to the death of the Medicis!

THE GUESTS *(They stand and drink)*: To the death of the Medicis!

LUISA *(She sets down her glass)*: Oh God! I'm sick!

FILIPPO: What's the matter, my darling? My dearest daughter, what is it? What's the matter? My God, how pale you are! What's the matter, tell Daddy. Help! Get help! Get the doctor!

LUISA: I'm going to die, I'm going to die. *(She falls)*

FILIPPO: She's dying! Get the doctor! They've poisoned my daughter! *(He falls to his knees beside Luisa)*

A GUEST: Make her drink some warm water; if it's poison, you need warm water.

The servants come running.

ANOTHER GUEST: Slap her wrists! Open the windows, and slap her wrists!

ANOTHER GUEST: Maybe she only fainted, she drank too much at once.

ANOTHER GUEST: She can't be dead so suddenly, just like that!

FILIPPO: My child! Luisa, my dear, my daughter, are you dead? Are you dead?

A GUEST: Here comes the doctor.

Enter a doctor.

ANOTHER GUEST: Quick, quick, tell us, is it poison?

FILIPPO: She's only fainted, hasn't she?

THE DOCTOR: The poor girl is dead.

Deep silence. Filippo is still on his knees beside Luisa, holding her hand.

A GUEST: This is Medici poison.

ANOTHER GUEST: I'm sure you're right. There was a serving woman near the table who used to work for the Salviatis.

ANOTHER GUEST: Salviati must have done it. Let's go; we can have him arrested.

ANOTHER GUEST: That Salviati wasn't after Luisa for himself; he was pimping for the Duke.

ANOTHER GUEST: Yes, let's get the Duke! Let's get Alessandro! He must have ordered all this. He's always hated us!

ANOTHER GUEST: Come on, let's go, before they murder us all.

FILIPPO *(He gets up)*: My friends, will you bury my daughter for me? *(He puts on his cloak)* In the garden. Behind the fig trees. Good night, my friends, my good friends, good night. Be well.

A GUEST: Where are you going, Filippo?

FILIPPO: It's too much for me, you see that, don't you, it's too much for me to bear. My two boys are in prison, and here's my girl dead. It's too much for me, I must go away.

ANOTHER GUEST: Go away? Without taking revenge?

FILIPPO: Yes, yes. Dress my poor girl for the grave, some poor monks I know will come fetch her tomorrow. Why do you look at her? She's dead, so it won't do any good, you understand. Good night, my friends, go home, go home, be well.

ANOTHER GUEST: Don't let him leave, his mind is beginning to wander.

Several guests try to restrain Filippo.

ANOTHER GUEST: How horrible! This room is
beginning to make me sick. *(He leaves)*

FILIPPO: Don't hurt me, don't leave me alone here, don't
shut me up in this room with that body. Let me go.

ANOTHER GUEST: Revenge, Filippo! Let us help you
take revenge. Your Luisa will be our Lucretia. We
will make Alessandro drink the rest of his poison.

ANOTHER GUEST: A second Lucretia! Let us all swear
on her body to die for freedom.

FILIPPO: Freedom, revenge, yes, of course, that's all very
beautiful. My two boys are in prison, and here's my
daughter dead. If I stay here, everyone around me
will die; the important thing is for me to go away. I
am old, you see that, don't you, it's time for me to
close up shop. Good night, my friends, don't worry, I
am going to Venice. Once I'm gone, no one will do
anything to you.

ANOTHER GUEST: There's a terrible storm beginning to
break; stay here tonight at least.

FILIPPO: My poor daughter. Tomorrow the monks will
come, they will take her away. Oh God of justice!
God of justice! What did I ever do to you? *(He leaves,
and begins to run)*

SCENE FIVE

The Duke's palace. Enter the Duke and Lorenzo.

THE DUKE: I wish I'd been there; the looks on their faces
must have been something. But why would anyone
want to poison Luisa?

LORENZO: I can't imagine. Unless it was you.

THE DUKE: Filippo must be going crazy. Somebody said he left for Venice. Thank God, I thought I'd never get rid of that impossible old man. Now maybe his family will mind their own business. Do you know they almost caused a riot in their neighborhood? They killed two of my German guards.

LORENZO: The thing that bothers me most is that your good friend Salviati has a broken leg. Did you ever find your chain mail?

THE DUKE: No. And by Christ, if I ever find out who took it . . .

LORENZO: You keep an eye on that Giomo. Who else could have taken it? What are you wearing instead?

THE DUKE: Nothing. I tried on some others, but they're all too heavy, I couldn't stand them. Now. I want to know what you found out about your cousin.

LORENZO: She's crazy about you. Ever since the red planet of your love has risen in her sky, she hasn't had a single night's sleep. You can tell from the look in her eyes. Have some pity on her, make a date for tonight, and let her make you a present of what little virginity she has left.

THE DUKE: Are you serious?

LORENZO: As serious as Death itself. I'd like to know why any cousin of mine wouldn't go to bed with you.

THE DUKE: Where can I meet her?

LORENZO: In my room. I'll have them put clean sheets on the bed and a pot of passion flowers on the bedroom table. I guarantee she'll be waiting for you, ready to go. And that'll keep you from getting bored after dinner, won't it?

THE DUKE: You can believe it. Goddam! Your Caterina is

a royal piece! Wait a minute, smart boy, what makes you sure she'll be there? How did you arrange all this?

LORENZO: I'll tell you later.

THE DUKE: Then come get me after dinner, we can go to your place together. And forget about that Cibo bitch, I've had it up to here with her. Yesterday she was on my back the whole afternoon. Good night, lover. *(He leaves)*

LORENZO: Now everything's taken care of. Tonight I'll take him to my room, and tomorrow the people who have been screaming for a republic can get to work, because the Duke of Florence will be dead. *(He leaves)*

SCENE SIX

A street. Enter Piero and Tommaso, returning from prison.

PIERO: I was sure the Council of Eight would let me go, and you too. There was no way they could hold us. Come on, I can't wait to tell Father. That's funny, all the shutters are closed.

They knock.

THE DOORMAN *(He opens the door)*: Oh, sir, you don't know what happened!

PIERO: What do you mean, what happened? You look like a ghost, and this place looks like a tomb.

THE DOORMAN: Didn't anyone tell you?

Two monks enter.

TOMMASO: How could anyone tell us anything? We just got out of prison.

THE DOORMAN: Oh, you poor boys, such a terrible thing . . .

THE MONKS: Is this the Strozzi palace?

THE DOORMAN: It is; who are you looking for?

ONE OF THE MONKS: We've come for the body of Luisa Strozzi. Here's a letter from Filippo, he authorizes you to release the body to us.

PIERO: What did you say? Whose body?

ONE OF THE MONKS: My son, you look too much like old Filippo, this isn't news you want to hear.

TOMMASO: Luisa's body? Is she dead? Dead? Oh my God, my God! *(He begins to cry, and sits down to one side)*

PIERO: Who killed my sister? Don't tell me she died naturally! Overnight? At her age? Who killed her? I'll kill him! Tell me, before I kill you too!

THE DOORMAN: How can I tell you? No one knows.

PIERO: Where's my father? Tommaso, stop crying. We must be hard now. Hard as stone.

THE MONKS: If you are Filippo's son, come with us, we'll take you to him. He's been at our monastery since yesterday.

PIERO: Won't any of you tell me who killed my sister? Listen to me, you priests, you are God's servants, you can witness a solemn oath: I swear by all the whips and chains of this world, by all the bloody instruments of hell. . . . No. Words won't work. Don't talk to me, don't say a word. I have a vengeance in me that will astonish the anger of God.

They exit.

SCENE SEVEN

A street. Enter Lorenzo and Scoronconcolo.

LORENZO: Go home and wait. Come to my house at
midnight, and stay in my study with the door locked
until I send you word. At midnight, remember.

SCORONCONCOLO: I will, Master. *(He leaves)*

LORENZO: Did my mother dream of tigers while she
carried me? Oh God, why do those words "at
midnight" burn my bones like a hot knife? What hairy
grappling conceived me, what animal guts gave me
birth? And what did that man ever do to me? When I
announce tomorrow that I've killed the Duke,
everyone will ask me "why?" What did he ever do to
me? And yet for this one act I abandoned everything.
It was as if I heard a crow at the side of the road call
kill him, kill him, kill him, and once the thought
occurred to me, my life has meant nothing. Why can't
I think about something else for a change? What am
I, the long arm of God? When I go into that bedroom
and draw my weapon, will it burst into flame like the
sword of the archangel? Will I fall upon his body like
a rain of ashes? *(He leaves)*

SCENE EIGHT

*The palace of the Marchese Cibo. Enter the Cardinal and the Mar-
chesa.*

MARCHESA: As you wish, Malaspina.

CARDINAL: Exactly. As I wish. Think twice the next

time, Marchesa, before you try to play games with
me. What are you, just another stupid female? Do you
need a badge and a warrant before you understand
my power? I am more than just the Pope's envoy or
the Emperor's ambassador, much more, believe me.

MARCHESA: Oh, I do believe you. The Emperor has sold
his shadow to the devil, and that shadow walks
around in red and answers to the name Cibo.

CARDINAL: You are Alessandro's mistress, remember
that. And your secret is in my hands.

MARCHESA: So then, you know my secret. Now what?

CARDINAL: Why was the Duke so eager to leave you this
afternoon? He looked like a schoolboy waiting for the
bell to ring at recess. What did you do, feed him the
stale patriotism you serve at all your dinner parties?
Didn't you ever learn that a Duke's mistress is
supposed to talk about other things than politics?

MARCHESA: Oh, I confess; I never learned exactly what a
Duke's mistress is supposed to talk about; no one
ever told me, and I forgot to ask.

CARDINAL: A woman doesn't need much learning to
know how to keep a man for more than three days.

MARCHESA: A woman needs a priest to teach her these
things, I gather. What would you have suggested I do?

CARDINAL: You want my suggestions? Good. Go change
your clothes, go to the palace and get into the Duke's
bed. If all he's been getting from you is speech-
making, prove to him you know how to do a few
others things as well. Just shut your eyes and do it,
and do it so that when he finally falls asleep on your
Republican bosom, it won't be out of sheer boredom.
What are you anyway, still a virgin? Don't we import
good wine anymore? Where's your copy of Aretino?

Haven't you read any dirty books lately?

MARCHESA: Good God. You talk like those filthy old
   ladies who pimp in the marketplace! If you can't act
   like a priest, can't you at least act like a man? You
   make your own red cassock blush for shame!

CARDINAL: How easy it is to shock the ears of an
   adulterous wife! If you want to pretend you don't
   understand me, go right ahead. Just remember, the
   man you married is my brother.

MARCHESA: Why won't you let me alone, that's what I
   can't understand. What's in all this for you? What are
   you hatching for me in that dark brain?

CARDINAL: I can't tell you, because I can't trust you. But
   I hope you realize that another woman in your place
   would have been a duchess by now. Don't you
   understand the power of a woman's smile? Alessandro
   is the Pope's son, remember that; and when the Pope
   met the Emperor in Bologna, he. . . . No. I've said too
   much already.

MARCHESA: Be careful, now it's you who are confessing.
   You may be my husband's brother, but I am
   Alessandro's mistress.

CARDINAL: So you are, Marchesa, and so were many
   other women before you.

MARCHESA: So they were. (To herself) And so was I—was,
   thank God. I was.

CARDINAL: Now listen to me, there's no reason for us to
   be at odds with each other. Really, you take things so
   seriously. Go get Alessandro back. I offended you just
   now by suggesting how to do it, so I won't offend you
   further if I repeat my suggestions. Do what I tell you;
   in a year or two you'll thank me. I have worked for a
   long time to get where I am, and I know what these

affairs can lead to. If I trusted you, I could tell you things God himself doesn't know.

MARCHESA: Don't count on me. I have nothing but contempt for you. *(She tries to leave)*

CARDINAL: Wait a minute. Not so fast. Isn't my brother due home today or tomorrow? Do you think I don't mean what I say? Go see the Duke at the palace tonight, or I will destroy you!

MARCHESA: Look, I understand, you're ambitious, you'll do anything to get what you want, I know all that, but what is it that you want? You never say what you mean! Believe me, Malaspina, I've gone this far, I don't want it all to have been for nothing! If you can convince me, talk. Talk! What is it you want?

CARDINAL: You've gone this far, but not far enough to do what I tell you, is that it? What do you think I am, a baby? You act first, I'll talk later. The day you tell me you have him in your power, and I don't mean Alessandro the Duke of Florence, I mean Alessandro the man, your lover, then I'll tell you what I have in mind.

MARCHESA: You mean that once I've read Aretino to get me through my first depravities, I can get through the next ones by reading the dirty little book of your mind? Shall I tell you, right now, what it is you don't dare tell me? You're the Pope's hatchet man, and you're waiting for the day the Emperor realizes you're a better hatchet man than the Pope himself. You're waiting for the day when all Italy will belong to the Emperor, because you intend to be the man who delivers it to him, and on that day, oh, I'm right, aren't I, on the day the Emperor takes over half the world he might just as well deliver over the Papal tiara and the keys of heaven to you. You want to control Florence by controlling the Duke, and you'd turn yourself into a woman right this minute to do it, if you could manage it. Instead you use me. That's it, isn't it? My imagination is as fertile as yours, believe me, but I think that's just about it.

CARDINAL: Go see the Duke tonight, or I'll destroy you.

MARCHESA: Destroy me? How?

The sound of horses and shouts in the courtyard below. The Cardinal goes to the window.

CARDINAL: You hear that? It's your husband. He's home. You think I won't tell him what you've been up to?

MARCHESA: Do it, go ahead and do it, I'll kill myself if you do!

CARDINAL: Women always say that. Listen to me. Whatever you may think I have in mind, you go spend tonight with the Duke.

MARCHESA: No.

CARDINAL: I swear to God I'll tell your husband everything if you say no to me again!

MARCHESA: No, no, no!

Enter the Marchese Cibo.

Lorenzo, while you were gone I went to bed with Alessandro, I had an affair with him, and I knew what I was doing, and how disgusting it all was. But this priest wants me to do something even more disgusting, he wants me to be the Duke's mistress so he can profit by it. *(She falls at the Marchese's feet)*

THE MARCHESE: Are you sick? What does she mean,

Malaspina? Well? You stand there like a statue. Is this some comedy you're playing, Cardinal? Well? What am I supposed to think?

CARDINAL: Jesus Christ! *(He leaves)*

THE MARCHESE: She's fainted. Somebody help!

SCENE NINE

Lorenzo's bedroom. Lorenzo and two servants.

LORENZO: Put these flowers beside the bed, and light a fire, but a fire with no flames, you understand? Only burning coals, that cast no light. Then give me the key, and go to bed.

The servants leave. Enter Caterina.

CATERINA: Your mother is sick, Renzo. Won't you come see her?

LORENZO: My mother is sick?

CATERINA: I have to tell you what happened. Yesterday the Duke wrote me a letter, what he said was, you were supposed to talk to me about . . . about making love with him. Your mother was very upset when she heard about it.

LORENZO: But I never did talk to you about . . . about that. Why couldn't you have told her I had nothing to do with it?

CATERINA: I did tell her. Why, you've cleaned up your room! And all these flowers! I thought you liked living in a mess.

LORENZO: The Duke wrote you? Funny, he didn't tell me

about it. Anyway . . . what do you think of his letter?

CATERINA: What do I think of it?

LORENZO: Yes. Alessandro has declared his intentions.
What does my innocent little cousin think of all that?

CATERINA: What do you expect me to think?

LORENZO: Weren't you flattered? Lots of women would
be, they'd love to be in your position, they'd do
whatever they had to in order to be the Duke's
mistress— *(He pauses)* Caterina, get out. Go tell my
mother I'll be there soon. Get out! Leave me alone!

Caterina leaves.

My God, am I a feather in every wind? Corruption
sticks to me, it's become part of myself, my skin, I can't
even control my tongue, I open my mouth and only filth
comes out. I wanted to seduce Caterina, I'd seduce my
own mother if the idea stuck in my head. Oh God, my
mind is a drawn bow, and the arrows it lets fly are
lethal. Poor Caterina! And yet you would die the way
Luisa Strozzi died, or end up worse, like all the rest, if
I weren't here to protect you. God, make sure Alessandro says his prayers before he walks into this room
tonight! *(He leaves)*

SCENE TEN

A valley, with a monastery in the distance. Enter Filippo Strozzi and two monks. Younger monks carry Luisa's coffin; they lower it into the tomb.

FILIPPO: Let me kiss her before you put her to bed for
the last time. I used to kiss her good night like this
after she'd gotten into bed, and then in the morning
she would come smiling to greet me, to return my
kiss of the night before. She brought a daily beauty to
my life, and made me welcome the shining morning.

They close the tomb.

PIERO *(Offstage)*: This way, it's over this way.

FILIPPO: And she will never get up again, never come to
find me in the morning. Oh, Luisa! You belong to
God now, and not to me, me, me!

PIERO *(As he enters)*: Filippo, there are a hundred men at
Sestino, just arrived from the Piedmont. We have no
time for tears.

FILIPPO: What do you know about time for tears?

PIERO: The exiles have gathered at Sestino, it's time to
think of revenge. We have a small army, we will
march directly on Florence. If we can get there before
morning and surprise the guards at the Citadel, it
will all be over. Then, by Christ, I intend to build my
sister a better tomb than this one!

FILIPPO: No, not I. Go on without me, friends.

PIERO: But we can't do it without you. You know that
everyone involved in this is counting on your

influence. Look, the King of France himself has written you a letter: Francis the First expects you to make the first move toward liberty.

FILIPPO *(He looks at the letter)*: Tell whoever gave you this to go back to the King of France and say: the day Filippo Strozzi takes up arms against his country, you can arrest him as a dangerous lunatic.

PIERO: Where did this new attitude come from all of a sudden?

FILIPPO: The attitude is my own.

PIERO: You'd abandon the exiles' cause just for the pleasure of a pose? Be careful, Father, you're not translating Roman history anymore. Think before you say no.

FILIPPO: I have known for sixty years what to reply to this letter from the King of France.

PIERO: I can't believe you've changed your mind! It's time somebody told you a few things!—Father, I beg of you, come with us. When I was on my way to meet the Pazzis, didn't you beg me to take you along? Is this any different?

FILIPPO: Very different. This is armed rebellion!

PIERO: It's a matter of revenge! A matter of getting rid of Alessandro! What's so different today? If you love your country, you won't let an occasion like this slip away!

FILIPPO: An occasion like this! Oh God, an occasion like this! *(He pounds against the tomb)*

PIERO: Change your mind. Come with us.

FILIPPO: My sorrow has no ambition in it. Leave me alone, I've told you all I can tell you.

PIERO: You stupid old man! You read too many books! If

we fail, it'll be your fault!

FILIPPO: Don't you talk to me like that, boy! Get out of here! Leave me alone!

PIERO: You do what you want! This time we'll act without you. Jesus Christ! No one's going to say that we lost everything just because a goddam translator changed his mind! *(He leaves)*

FILIPPO: Judgment is at hand, Filippo! The signs are all here, your day of judgment is at hand!

SCENE ELEVEN

Evening; the embankment of the Arno River. A row of palaces.

LORENZO: The sun has almost set. No time to lose. Even here in a city where there's nothing to lose anymore but time. *(He knocks at a door)* Hey! Signor Alamanno! Hey!

ALAMANNO *(He appears at his window)*: Who's there? What do you want?

LORENZO: I came to let you know that the Duke is going to be killed tonight. Get your friends together and prepare for tomorrow, if you want freedom.

ALAMANNO: Alessandro? Killed? By who?

LORENZO: By me, Lorenzo Medici.

ALAMANNO: Is that you, Lorenzaccio? Come and have a drink with us! We're having a party.

LORENZO: I haven't got time. Be ready to act tomorrow.

ALAMANNO: *You're* going to kill the Duke? Forget it! You've had too much to drink! *(He goes inside)*

LORENZO: Maybe I shouldn't tell them it's me who's going to do it; nobody believes me. *(He knocks at another door)* Hey! Signor Pazzi! Hey!

PAZZI *(He appears at his window)*: Who's that?

LORENZO: I came to tell you that the Duke is going to be killed tonight. Get ready to act tomorrow for the sake of freedom in Florence.

PAZZI: Who's going to kill the Duke?

LORENZO: It's not important who. The important thing is, be ready to act! Get your friends together.

PAZZI: You must be crazy. Go to hell. *(He goes inside)*

LORENZO: Wonderful. If I don't tell them it's me, they believe me even less. *(He knocks at another door)* Hey! Signor Corsini!

CORSINI *(He appears at his window)*: What's the matter?

LORENZO: Duke Alessandro is going to be killed tonight.

CORSINI: Oh, really. Who's that, Lorenzo? You're drunk. Go make a scene someplace else. You gave me enough trouble the other night at Nasi's party. You can go to hell for all I care. *(He goes inside)*

LORENZO: Oh, Florence! Florence! No one believes me!

He sits down near the water's edge. It has grown dark.

But *he* believes me. I've convinced him. I've played my part perfectly. All we have left to play is the final scene. And *I* set the stage. I'll put out the light . . . that's ordinary, people do it all the time. . . . I'll tell him she's shy . . . a new bride, for instance, she'd tell her husband to put out the light . . .

Anyway, what's done is done. I've got to stay calm! It's only an hour, and the clock just struck. . . . Oh, God! Who'll believe he's really dead? None of them, not even Filippo!

The full moon appears in the sky.

Is that you, whiteface? If a single one of these Friends
of the Republic had any guts, what a revolution you'd
see in this city tomorrow! But Piero is only out for
himself, and the rest. . . . Oh, words, words, nothing
but language! Are you alone up there? If there is anyone there with you, he must be laughing his head off at
us! It's funny, all this, isn't it, really funny! All of
humanity talking, talking talking. . . . And not a man in
the world is willing to act!

   No! No, I won't put out the light! I'll go right for his
heart, he can watch as I kill him! Oh Christ Jesus! And
tomorrow they'll open all their windows, and how they
will stare! If only he doesn't have a new chain mail,
suppose he got another one somewhere . . . damn all
armor anyway! He'll go in first, I'll follow him; he'll put
down his sword there . . . or maybe there . . . yes, over
there, on the bench . . . and then I'll wrap the swordbelt
around the scabbard, that's easy. The easiest thing
would be if he decided to get into bed right away . . .
lying down, or standing up? Lying down, that's best. I'll
go out for a minute, Scoronconcolo will be in the next
room. Then we come in, we come in . . . just as long as
he doesn't turn his back. I'll go straight for him. . . . All
right, that's enough, that's enough! It's not time yet! I
need a drink, it's cold out. No, I don't want to drink
tonight. Where the hell am I? Anyway, the bars are all
closed.

   (*He imitates a conversation*) "Is she a virgin?" "Oh,
absolutely!" "Is she naked?" "Oh, I don't think so, not
yet. . . . " Poor Caterina! And all this may kill my

mother, that's too bad. . . . But she'd just . . . suppose I did tell her what I was going to do, she'd just shout "Criminal!" at me, and then she'd die. Why do I keep walking like this, I'm worn out. *(He collapses onto a bench)*

Filippo! His daughter was as beautiful as the dawn! I remember once I sat next to her under the trees in his garden, I watched her sewing, I watched her little white hands. . . . Under the trees, all those days I spent under the trees, how peaceful it was!

A clock strikes.

Oh! Oh! It's time, time to act! The play begins! "Oh, it's you, lover, sit down and have a drink! Have a little drink with Giomo! How's the wine, good?" "Oh yes, good!" And wouldn't it be funny if he asked me whether the bedroom was quiet, and if the neighbors could hear anything!

I feel like dancing! If I let myself go I could fly like a bird! Oh, lover, lover! Yes, put on your good clothes, put on your best clothes, you want to look good for your wedding night, the bride is very beautiful! But let me tell you a secret, lover, let me whisper in your ear, lover: watch out! The bride may have a knife! *(He leaves at a run)*

SCENE TWELVE

The Duke's palace. The Duke is eating supper. Giomo pours wine. Enter Cardinal Cibo.

CARDINAL: Highness, be careful of Lorenzo.

THE DUKE: Oh, it's you, Cardinal. Sit down and have a drink.

CARDINAL: Be careful of Lorenzo. He went to the Bishop of Marzi tonight to ask for post horses. Fast ones.

THE DUKE: He did not.

CARDINAL: The Bishop himself told me he did.

THE DUKE: I don't care who told you; I'm telling you he didn't, for one very good reason which I happen to know.

CARDINAL: I doubt it will convince me; but at least I've warned you, so I've done my duty.

THE DUKE: Even if it were true, what's so scary about that? Maybe he wants to go to his place in the country.

CARDINAL: What's so scary about it, Highness, is that on my way here I saw him with my own eyes jumping around on the riverbank like a madman. I called to him, and he looked at me, and the look in his face made me afraid. He has something planned for this evening, believe me.

THE DUKE: And why should his plans worry me?

CARDINAL: Must I spell everything out? I know the two of you are . . . very close. But two people I know personally have informed me that he told them, this evening, in public, right in front of their houses, that he intends to kill you tonight.

THE DUKE: Cardinal, have another drink. Don't you know Renzo is always drunk by sunset?

Enter Sior Maurizio.

SIOR MAURIZIO: Highness, watch out for Lorenzo. He's told three different friends of mine that he intends to kill you tonight.

THE DUKE: You too, Maurizio? You listen to fairy tales? I thought you were too much of a man for that.

SIOR MAURIZIO: Your Highness knows I don't take precautions without good reason. I can prove what I just said.

THE DUKE: Oh, sit down and have a drink with the Cardinal. But I hope you'll both excuse me, I've got other plans.

Enter Lorenzo.

Well, lover? Is it time to go?

LORENZO: It's just after midnight.

THE DUKE: Bring me my silk jacket.

LORENZO: Hurry up; the lady must be ready and waiting by now.

THE DUKE: What about gloves? What do you think I should wear: pigskin or kidskin?

LORENZO: Oh, kidskin, Highness. This one is definitely kidskin.

THE DUKE: Good, I'm in the mood for something soft and smooth.

They leave.

SIOR MAURIZIO: Well, Cardinal, what do you think?
CARDINAL: We've done what we can. The rest is up to
    God, not us.

They leave.

SCENE THIRTEEN

Lorenzo's room. Enter the Duke and Lorenzo.

THE DUKE: It's freezing in here! It's a good thing you
    had them make a fire.

He takes off his sword; Lorenzo takes it.

What do you want with that, lover?
LORENZO: I'm tying your belt around your sword, and
    I'm going to put it right here, under the bed. You
    never know when you'll need it. *(He ties the belt
    around the sword so it can't be drawn from the scabbard)*
THE DUKE: Someone told me Caterina likes to talk. You
    know I can't stand women who talk. Maybe I'll just
    get right into bed, that ought to discourage
    conversation. Oh, I forgot. There was something I
    wanted to ask you. Why did you ask the Bishop of
    Marzi for a set of fast horses?
LORENZO: So I could go see my brother, he's in bed.
    Sick. At least that's what he wrote me.
THE DUKE: Go get your cousin.
LORENZO: I'll be right back. *(He leaves)*

THE DUKE: I hate making small talk with a woman who's already decided to say yes. It's dumb. Anyway, I drank so much tonight I couldn't give the time of day to the Spanish Infanta if I wanted to. I'll just get into bed and pretend I'm asleep. Maybe that's crude, but it saves time. *(He gets into bed)*

Enter Lorenzo, a sword in his hand.

LORENZO: Asleep already, Highness? *(He stabs him)*
THE DUKE: Lorenzo! You?
LORENZO: Me, Highness. Lorenzo. Believe it.

He stabs him again; they struggle. Enter Scoronconcolo.

SCORONCONCOLO: Is he dead?
LORENZO: Look. He bit my finger. I'll wear this mark till I die, like a diamond ring.
SCORONCONCOLO: Jesus Christ! It's the Duke!
LORENZO *(He goes to the window)*: What a beautiful night! The air is clean at last! *(He takes a deep breath)*
SCORONCONCOLO: Master! Sir! We've done too much! Let's go!
LORENZO: Smell the evening air! How sweet it is! What a wonderful place the world is, all of a sudden! I feel now I could sleep forever!
SCORONCONCOLO: The wind is cold; it's beginning to freeze the sweat on your forehead. Sir! Let's go!
LORENZO: God *is* good! Now I know!
SCORONCONCOLO: He's crazy. I've got to get out of here! *(He starts to leave)*
LORENZO: Wait a minute! Close the window! Close the curtains! Give me the key to the room.

SCORONCONCOLO: I just hope no one heard anything.
LORENZO: Have you forgotten already? No one has ever heard anything from this room but screams.

They leave.

SCENE FOURTEEN

The Duke's palace, next morning. Enter Valori, Sior Maurizio, and Guicciardini. A crowd of courtiers moves about the room and the hallway outside.

SIOR MAURIZIO: Giomo still isn't back yet. This whole business is getting more and more upsetting.
GUICCIARDINI: Here he comes now.

Enter Giomo.

SIOR MAURIZIO: All right, what did you find out?
GIOMO: Nothing. *(He goes out)*
GUICCIARDINI: He won't tell us. Cardinal Cibo is in the Duke's office, everyone is reporting to him.

A messenger enters.

You! What's happened? Have they found the Duke?
MESSENGER: I don't know. *(He goes into the Duke's office)*
VALORI: What a terrible thing, gentlemen, the Duke gone, disappeared, and no one knows where! Didn't you say you'd seen him last night, Sior Maurizio? Did he seem sick to you?

Giomo comes back in.

GIOMO *(Whispering to Sior Maurizio)*: Now I can tell you. The Duke has been murdered.

SIOR MAURIZIO: Murdered? Who did it? Where did you find him?

GIOMO: Exactly where you told us to look. In Lorenzo's bedroom.

SIOR MAURIZIO: Goddam it! Does the Cardinal know?

GIOMO: Yes, Excellency.

SIOR MAURIZIO: What did he say? What should we do? We're dead men if the people find out. There's already a crowd of people heading toward the palace. They'll tear us to pieces.

Servants can be seen in the background, carrying cases of wine and platters of food.

GUICCIARDINI: What's all this about? Are they going to distribute that to the crowd?

A lord approaches.

A LORD: Will the Duke put in an appearance today, gentlemen? This is a cousin of mine, just arrived from Germany, I'd like to introduce him to His Highness; I hope you'll give him your support.

GUICCIARDINI: You talk to him, Valori, I don't know what to say.

VALORI: The room is full of people who've been here since this morning. They're all waiting to see the Duke.

SIOR MAURIZIO *(To Giomo)*: Did you bury him already?

GIOMO: Sure, right in the church next door. What else
could we do? If the people find out he's dead, there'll
be a few more of us dead before it's all over. We can
have a funeral when things ease up. Meanwhile we
rolled him up in a rug.

VALORI: What's to become of us now?

Several lords approach.

LORDS: Will we be able to see His Highness soon? What
do you suppose is going on, gentlemen?

Enter Cardinal Cibo.

CARDINAL: Gentlemen, gentlemen, the Duke will see
you in an hour or so. His Highness spent the night at
a costume party, and at the moment he is resting.

*Two servants hang up a masked costume on one of the arch-
ways.*

THE COURTIERS: We'll leave now, the Duke is still
asleep. He was out all night dancing.

The courtiers leave. Enter the members of the Council of Eight.

NICCOLINI: What's been decided, Cardinal?

CARDINAL: *Primo avulso, non deficit alter—Aureus, et simili
frondescrit virga metallo. (He leaves)*

NICCOLINI: That's easy enough for him to say, but what
are we supposed to do now? The Duke is dead, we
have to elect another one. If we don't have a new

Duke by this evening or tomorrow morning, it's all over for us. The people are a pot of water about to boil.

VETTORI: I propose Ottavio Medici.

CAPPONI: Why? He's not next in the line of succession.

ACCAIUOLI: Suppose we elected the Cardinal?

SIOR MAURIZIO: What kind of a joke is that supposed to be?

RUCCELLAI: Why a joke? You've let him take over so far, and he has no legal rights in this matter whatsoever.

VETTORI: Because he's a man who knows how to run things.

RUCCELLAI: He has to get the Pope's permission first.

VETTORI: He already has it; the Pope sent back his authorization by the same messenger the Cardinal sent to Rome last night.

RUCCELLAI: What did he send, a carrier pigeon? A messenger has to take the time to get to Rome before he can come back. What does he think we are, children?

CANIGIANI *(He approaches them)*: Gentlemen, if you want my advice, what we should do is elect Giuliano, the Duke's natural son.

RUCCELLAI: Oh, bravo! He's five years old! That's what you're proposing, isn't it, Canigiani, a five-year-old boy?

GUICCIARDINI *(Aside)*: Can't you see what he's up to? The Cardinal obviously put him up to this. That way Cibo becomes regent, and the boy can go on playing with his toy swords.

RUCCELLAI: That's scandalous and stupid. If this is the kind of proposal we intend to discuss, I'm leaving right now.

CORSI *(He enters)*: Gentlemen, the Cardinal has written to
Cosimo Medici.

THE EIGHT: Without consulting us?

CORSI: The Cardinal has also written to Pisa, to Arezzo,
and to Pistoia, to the military commanders there.
Giacomo Medici will be here tomorrow with the
largest force he can gather, and Alessandro Vitelli is
already in command of the Citadel. The entire
garrison is with him. And as for Lorenzo, three
detachments have been sent to stop him.

RUCCELLAI: Why doesn't he just make himself Duke
right this minute, this Cardinal of yours, it might
speed things up.

CORSI: He ordered me to request that you put the name
of Cosimo Medici to a vote, with the temporary rank
of Governor of the Republic of Florence.

A pause.

SIOR MAURIZIO: Come, come, gentlemen, it's time to
vote. Here are your ballots.

VETTORI: Well, after all, Cosimo is Alessandro's closest
relative, he should be next in line.

ACCAIUOLI: What kind of man is he? I know very little
about him.

CORSI: Oh, a true prince. He'll make an ideal ruler.

GUICCIARDINI: Heh-heh, not quite, not quite. If you
were to say, now, a tricky prince, the trickiest of
princes, I might agree with you.

SIOR MAURIZIO: Your votes, gentlemen.

RUCCELLAI: I want to state my formal opposition to this
vote, and I do it in the name of every citizen of
Florence.

VETTORI: Why?

RUCCELLAI: A republic has no need of princes, or of dukes, or of rulers at all. I abstain.

VETTORI: Your vote is one vote only. We can do without it.

RUCCELLAI: Then goodbye to you all. I wash my hands of the whole affair.

GUICCIARDINI *(Running after him)*: Palla, for godsakes, wait! You're overreacting!

RUCCELLAI: Let me alone! I'm almost seventy years old, there isn't much more you can do to me after this! *(He leaves)*

NICCOLINI: Your votes, gentlemen!

The ballots are collected; he unfolds them.

Unanimous. Has the courier left for Trebbio?

CORSI: He's gone already, Excellency. Cosimo should be here by tomorrow morning—assuming he doesn't refuse.

VETTORI: Refuse? Why would he want to refuse? We all voted, and there's no reason for him not to accept. This whole business stinks, anyway.

They leave.

SCENE FIFTEEN

A field. Enter Piero Strozzi and two exiles.

PIERO: My father won't come. And I couldn't persuade him.

FIRST EXILE: I can't tell that to my compadres. It's

enough to make them give up on the whole effort.

PIERO: Why? Start out tonight, and ride to Sestino as fast as you can; I'll be there tomorrow. Tell them Filippo won't come, but that Piero will.

FIRST EXILE: Our people want Filippo's name. We won't move without it.

PIERO: His name is the same as mine. Just tell them Strozzi is coming, that's all they need.

FIRST EXILE: They'll ask me which Strozzi, and if I don't tell them Filippo they won't do a thing.

PIERO: Do what I tell you and don't act like an asshole! How the hell do you know what they'll do or won't do? You just worry about what *you'll* do.

FIRST EXILE: I wouldn't talk to people that way, sir, if I were you.

PIERO: Go get your horse and ride to Sestino!

FIRST EXILE: Look, sir, my horse is tired. I've ridden twenty miles tonight. I don't feel like doing any more riding.

PIERO: You're an asshole! *(To the second exile)* All right, you, you go. At least you look like you know what you're doing.

SECOND EXILE: My compadre here is right about Filippo. He's the one we need to get people on our side.

PIERO: Fucking farmers! Where's your guts? Your goddam wives and children are starving and all you can talk about is Filippo, Filippo, Filippo! What kind of assholes are you anyway?

SECOND EXILE: I don't take language like that from anybody. *(To the first exile)* Come on, let's go.

They leave.

PIERO: Yeah, go! Go to hell, assholes! You go tell your
        friends if they don't want me, the King of France
        does! And tell them to watch out if they ever get in
        my way!

SCENE SIXTEEN

Venice. Filippo Strozzi in his study.

FILIPPO: I knew it. Piero is working for the King of
          France. He's put together an army of some kind, and
          is ready to attack his own city. So that is to be the
          accomplishment of the Strozzi family! A rebel in
          arms and a massacre! Oh, my poor Luisa! You at least
          have found peace, there beneath the grass where I left
          you. *(A knock at the door)* Come in.

Enter Lorenzo.

LORENZO: Filippo, I bring you the greatest gift you or I
          could ever imagine.
FILIPPO: What is this? A key?
LORENZO: The key to my bedroom. Open the door, and
          you will find the body of Alessandro de Medici. I
          murdered him. With this hand!
FILIPPO: Is that true? Is that true? I cannot believe it.
LORENZO: What would you say now if the Friends of the
          Republic came to make you Duke of Florence instead
          of him?
FILIPPO: My friend, I would refuse.
LORENZO: Is that true? Is that true? I cannot believe it.

FILIPPO: Why not? For me, that is a very simple thing to do.

LORENZO: And it was a very simple thing for me to kill Alessandro. Why won't you believe me?

FILIPPO *(He looks into his face)*: I do believe you! You are Brutus born again! Come, let me embrace you! Liberty lives! We are saved! The Duke is dead! I feel no hatred for him, as God is my witness, all I feel is love, love of country, the purest love in the world.

LORENZO: Calm down, calm down. The only thing saved is me, and my butt has been severely bruised by two days' ride on the Bishop of Marzi's horses.

FILIPPO: Have you told our friends? Did the Friends of the Republic rise to take control of the situation?

LORENZO: I told everybody in town. I even shouted it to the moon, to make sure at least someone heard me.

FILIPPO: What do you mean?

LORENZO: I mean that they all shrugged their shoulders and went right back to their dinners or their wives or whatever it was they were doing.

FILIPPO: But didn't you explain to them what was going to happen?

LORENZO: What the hell was there to explain? I didn't have an hour to waste on each of them. I told them all to get ready, and then I went and did what I said I would.

FILIPPO: Why didn't you go out into the streets with the Duke's head in your hand? The people would have hailed you as their savior and followed you anywhere.

LORENZO: I left the dead meat for the dogs. They can gut him themselves.

FILIPPO: You would love the people, if you didn't have such contempt for them.

LORENZO: I don't have contempt for them, I just know what they're like, that's all.

FILIPPO: Why say things like that, if you don't know what you're talking about? You can't deny the history of the whole world!

LORENZO: I don't deny history, but I wasn't there for it, so how should I know what happened?

FILIPPO: Then let me call you Brutus! If I am dreaming, don't take my dream away!

Shouts from outside.

What's that? There's a crowd gathering. Open the window.

LORENZO: No, Filippo. Don't open the window.

FILIPPO *(He goes to the window)*: Look down there, can't you see? A courier has arrived with the proclamation! *(He shouts down)* Giovanni, bring me a copy of that paper! My Brutus! My Lorenzo, Lorenzo the Great! The sky is full of Liberty, I can feel it with every breath I breathe!

LORENZO: Filippo, Filippo, close the window. You're making me sick.

FILIPPO: Listen, they must be reading the proclamation.

LORENZO: Oh God! Oh my God!

FILIPPO: You're pale as death; what's the matter?

LORENZO: Can't you hear what they're shouting?

Giovanni enters with a copy of the proclamation.

FILIPPO: No, but here's the proclamation, read it to me.

LORENZO *(He reads)*: "To any man who kills Lorenzo de Medici, traitor to his country and assassin of his sovereign Lord, in whatever part of Italy, the Council of Eight of Florence promises to pay, first, four thousand gold florins nontaxable; second, a hundred florins a year income as long as he lives; third, permission to hold any public office whatsoever, without regard to rank or status; four, unconditional pardon for any crimes past or future, great or small." Signed with the seal of the Eight. Well, Filippo, now do you believe that I killed Alessandro?

FILIPPO: Be quiet! Someone is coming up the stairs. You'd better hide.

They leave.

SCENE SEVENTEEN

A street in Florence by the shops of the jeweler and the silk merchant. The Marchese and the Marchesa pass in the distance. Enter two noblemen.

FIRST NOBLEMAN: Either I am crazy, or that is the Marchese Cibo! Arm in arm with his wife!

SECOND NOBLEMAN: The good Marchese obviously doesn't hold a grudge. Why, everyone in Florence knows his wife was the dead Duke's mistress.

FIRST NOBLEMAN: It certainly doesn't seem to have come between them. See how they smile at one another!

SECOND NOBLEMAN: The perfect husband! Now that's what I call a man with a good digestion, having to swallow a story as long and dirty as the Arno!

FIRST NOBLEMAN: Take my advice, don't bring up the

subject when he's around; he's a fighter. Make any smart remarks and you may wind up face down in the dirt of his famous garden.

SECOND NOBLEMAN: Well, if he can't take a joke, there isn't much to say, is there?

They leave. The jeweler and the silk merchant talk.

SILK MERCHANT: Pay attention, you hear what I'm saying? Alessandro was killed this year, right? All right, so he dies in the year 1536. And he's twenty-six years old, right? But that's not all: when does he get killed? On the sixth day of the month, did you notice that? I'm right, aren't I, he gets killed on the sixth, doesn't he? All right, now listen to this. He gets killed at six o'clock at night! What do you say to that, Mondella? He gets killed at six o'clock! Now wait a minute, wait a minute, there's more. He got stabbed six times. There! You get it? He got stabbed six times, at six o'clock, on the sixth, at the age of twenty-six, in the year 1536. Now—and this is the clincher: he was Duke for six years.

JEWELER: And just what the hell is all that supposed to mean?

SILK MERCHANT: What do you mean, what's it supposed to mean? Can't you count? Don't you see what it all adds up to?

JEWELER: I don't see that it adds up to anything. What do you think it means?

SILK MERCHANT: What it means is that three sixes—*two times*—were involved in Alessandro's death. Only don't tell anybody I told you. I'm not usually a superstitious man, I don't want people thinking I believe in that stuff. But I tell you right to your face, neighbor, man to man, three sixes is *evil*.

JEWELER: Evil? Look I may be an old man, but I'm not completely senile. What it adds up to is that today Cosimo arrives. What your three sixes gets us is another crooked politician overnight.

SILK MERCHANT: Some people say we should set up the Council the way it used to be, and elect a Gonfaloniere like we used to.

JEWELER: You're right, some people say that, but nobody does anything about it.

SILK MERCHANT: You know what else I heard? They say Roberto Corsini, the Commander of the Citadel, went to the Friends of the Republic meeting last night at the Salviati palace.

JEWELER: I know for a fact he did. He offered to turn over the Citadel to them, weapons, stockpiles, keys, everything.

SILK MERCHANT: Did he really do it? They could get him for treason for something like that!

JEWELER: Of course they could, but nothing happened! They were all afraid to do what he suggested, so they said he was just trying to trick them. Damn it, they make me mad, the whole bunch of them! Look over there, it's the messengers returned from Trebbio. Cosimo can't be far behind. Neighbor, I'm going to the palace. All this excitement has got my blood up.

SILK MERCHANT: Wait a minute, neighbor, I'm coming with you.

They leave. Enter a tutor in charge of the Salviati boy, and a second tutor in charge of the Strozzi boy.

FIRST TUTOR: My learned friend, delighted to see you, absolutely delighted. You are well, I hope, and not too badly put out by these tempestuous machinations in the body politic?

SECOND TUTOR: Not at all, and believe me the delight is mine, assuages this absolutely vociferous need to encounter a familiar face, or should I say rather a familiar voice, one with a sense of *sense*, if you know what I mean, in this desperate cacophony of ambiguities. You are, believe me, the magnificent exception to *that*, and I refer, of course, to your recent article on the problem of liberty and exigesis.

SALVIATI BOY: You pig-breath, Strozzi!

STROZZI BOY: Fuck your father, Salviati!

FIRST TUTOR: Ah, you did happen to see it then! Well, of course, the central problem follows your line of reasoning in "From bilateral literalism to free displacements in revolutionary narrativity," but I did hope to get at, you know, some of the thornier metaphysics, the old Aristotelian in-and-out, so to speak . . .

SECOND TUTOR: And you did, and you did, no question about it, even our highfalutin' friends at the University all agree, and I hear that a tiny *offer* may just be in the offing, if you know what I mean . . .

FIRST TUTOR: Of course I might be said to have mixed metaphors in midstream, I suppose, if you consider my previous work on "the Absolutes of Absolutism," and this new material may be just a teeny bit *contre-revanchiste,* even teetering on the brink of Republicanism, if you will . . .

SALVIATI BOY: Strozzi, you stink! Don't try to kick me, you . . .

STROZZI BOY: Suck this, Salviati! I'll kick your ass so fast . . .

FIRST TUTOR: . . . but I think I have successfully made the leap into the signifying *beyond* of discourse . . .

SALVIATI BOY: Sir, help me beat the shit out of this little pig-sticker, he's a pig-sticker, all the Strozzis are pig-stickers!

SECOND TUTOR: Now, now, mustn't fight.

STROZZI BOY: You coming back for more? Okay, asshole, here's for you, and this is for your father, tell him to stick it where Piero Strozzi stuck it to him, and he's a poison-murderer too, all you Salviatis are poison-murderers.

FIRST TUTOR: Shut up, you little bastard! *(He slaps the Strozzi boy)*

STROZZI BOY: Ow, ow! He hit me!

FIRST TUTOR: And so I think I may safely say that I am at that point where language dissolves and the bipolarities of radical politics become moot, if you see what I mean, even mooter than they might . . .

STROZZI BOY: Ow, ow! He hurt my ear!

SECOND TUTOR: You know, I think you hit him just a little bit too hard . . .

The Strozzi boy beats up the Salviati boy.

FIRST TUTOR: I don't think I made the slightest impression on him.

SECOND TUTOR: Anyway, as you were saying . . .

The two boys go out fighting, and the tutors follow them.

SCENE EIGHTEEN

A field. Enter Piero Strozzi and a messenger.

PIERO: Those were his own words?
THE MESSENGER: Yes, Excellency, those were the King's
very words.
PIERO: Good.

The messenger leaves.

The King of France out to protect the liberty of Italy,
that's good, that's wonderful. That's like a rapist
protecting a beautiful woman from another rapist. Well,
whatever happens, at least it's a way to begin, with more
to gain than to lose. But fuck that Lorenzaccio, who
only wanted to be famous! He tore my vengeance from
between my teeth! Now what's left to do that's worth
my doing it? Attack the city. I can attack the city, and
fuck all those faggots who wanted my father instead of
me! *(He leaves)*

SCENE NINETEEN

*Venice. Filippo Strozzi's study. Filippo, and Lorenzo reading a
letter.*

LORENZO: Filippo, my mother is dead. Come take a walk
with me, will you?
FILIPPO: My friend, you must not tempt fate this way!
You come and go as you please, just as if this
proclamation didn't exist.

LORENZO: It all fits. They put a price on my head in
        Rome when I tried to kill the Pope. Now that I've
        killed Alessandro, they put a price on it throughout
        Italy. If I left Italy I'm sure they'd proclaim the price
        all over Europe, and when I die I expect Almighty
        God will proclaim my eternal damnation on the
        billboards of the universe.

FILIPPO: You haven't changed, Lorenzo. Your jokes are
        still the saddest things in the world.

LORENZO: Not true. Oh, I wear the same clothes, I walk
        on the same two legs, I yawn with the same mouth,
        but one thing has changed. There's nothing inside
        me. I am as hollow as a broken drum.

FILIPPO: We must leave this country, both of us. You are
        still young in spite of all you've done; you can
        become a man again.

LORENZO: I am older than the Roman statues I smashed
        one night when I was drunk. Filippo, please, let's go
        for a walk.

FILIPPO: You have nothing to do, that's what's the matter.
        It's driving you crazy. Things are beginning to bother
        you.

LORENZO: Oh, I agree. The Friends of the Republic of
        Florence have accomplished nothing, that bothers me.
        A hundred students full of bravery and ideals got
        themselves beaten up and murdered and all for
        nothing, that bothers me. Our country cousin Cosimo
        was unanimously elected Duke, that bothers me a lot.
        Oh, you're right, you're right, a lot of things bother
        me, they bother the hell out of me!

FILIPPO: Let's not try to figure out what happened when
        it's not over yet. The important thing is for you to get
        out of Italy. You still have a life to live.

LORENZO: No, I was a murder machine, and a disposable murder machine. Use once, then throw away.

FILIPPO: Is this murder the only thing that has ever made you happy? Finally you have a chance to live an honest, ordinary life; I don't understand why you want to die.

LORENZO: All I can do, Filippo, is tell you what I've already told you: I was honest once. Maybe I'll be honest again and maybe it won't bore me. I still like to drink, I suppose I still like girls; that's enough to make a sinner of me, but it's not enough to make me want to be one. Let's go, please.

FILIPPO: You'll get yourself killed on these walks of yours.

LORENZO: It makes me laugh to see the people who follow me. The reward for my death is so enormous it almost makes them brave. And none of them dares do anything! Anyway, I don't care what they do. I'm going down to the Rialto. *(He leaves)*

FILIPPO: He needs protection. Hey! Giovanni! Pippo! Hey!

Enter a servant.

Go get your swords, you and one of the other boys, and follow Lorenzo. Keep a decent distance, but be ready to defend him in case he's attacked.

GIOVANNI: Yes, sir.

Shouts in the street below. Filippo goes to the window. Enter Pippo.

PIPPO: Sir, Lorenzo is dead. There was a man hiding near the front door, he stabbed him in the dark on his way out.

FILIPPO: Hurry! Go get him! He may be only wounded.

PIPPO: Can't you see how many people have gathered?
    The whole crowd has attacked Lorenzo. Good Christ.
    They're hacking his body. Look! They've thrown him
    into the canal!

FILIPPO: Oh, God of Justice! Not even a body left to bury!

SCENE TWENTY

Florence, the Piazza della Signoria. Crowds of people. At a balcony window, Cosimo de Medici and Cardinal Cibo.

THE PEOPLE: Long live the Medicis! Hurrah! A Medici
    Duke! A Medici Duke!

SOLDIERS: Out of the way, scum!

CARDINAL: Sir, you are now Duke of Florence. Before
    receiving this crown which the Pope and the Emperor
    have charged me to confer upon you, I am directed to
    request you to swear to four things.

COSIMO: What are they, Cardinal?

CARDINAL: To bring justice for all, without distinction;
    never to rebel against the authority of the Emperor
    Charles the Fifth; to revenge the death of
    Alessandro; and to care for his natural children
    Giulio and Giuliana.

COSIMO: How do you want me to swear?

CARDINAL: On the Bible. *(He holds out a Bible)*

COSIMO: I so solemnly swear, before God, and before
    you, Cardinal. *(He leans out the window to address the
    crowd)* "Most noble and powerful Lords, I can best
    thank the illustrious noble families of Florence for
    the title they have bestowed upon me by swearing

before you all, young as I am, to keep the fear of God always before me, and in my government always to keep in mind the advice and consent of the noble families of Florence, whom I here publicly acknowledge and commend."

The crowd cheers loudly.

You Can't Think of Everything

TRANSLATED BY
MICHAEL FEINGOLD

The Marquis of Valberg

The Baron

Germain, the Marquis' valet

The Countess of Vernon

Victoria, her maid

The Countess's chateau in the country.

TRANSLATOR'S NOTE

This translation was made possible by a grant from the National Endowment for the Arts, under a program now discontinued. The translator gratefully acknowledges the assistance of the Endowment's Theater Program and its former staff.

The translation was first produced at La Mama E.T.C. in December 1989. It is dedicated to Daniel Pardo, first and most endearingly absent-minded of Valbergs.

The Baron, Germain.

BARON: You say my nephew's nowhere to be found?

GERMAIN: No, sir; I've looked for him everywhere.

BARON: That's impossible; it's exactly five o'clock. This is the Countess's house, isn't it?

GERMAIN: Yes, sir; there's her piano.

BARON: Perhaps my nephew doesn't love her anymore?

GERMAIN: Oh, yes, sir, as usual.

BARON: And he does come to see her every day?

GERMAIN: Sir, it's the only thing he does do.

BARON: Perhaps he didn't get my letter?

GERMAIN: I'm sure he did, sir, this very morning.

BARON: Then since he wasn't at home, he must be somewhere in this house. I informed him emphatically that I was leaving Paris at one-thirty, and as a result I would arrive at his estate by three. From his estate to here is seven-and-a-half miles. Seven-and-a-half miles, estimate an hour and a quarter, assuming the roads are bad—though in actual fact they aren't bad at all—

GERMAIN: On the contrary, they're especially good right now.

BARON: I left his estate at three, and as a result I must definitely have reached the inn here at four-fifteen. I had to pay a visit to Milord Duplessis, which could not possibly have lasted longer than fifteen minutes. So, with the time it would take me to get here from the inn, I couldn't have arrived here any later than five p.m., plus a few minutes' waiting time. Are my calculations accurate?

GERMAIN: Perfectly, sir; but my master is not here.

BARON: Has he packed his bags, at least?

GERMAIN: Begging your pardon, sir, what bags?

BARON: I mean is his luggage ready, back at his chateau?

GERMAIN: Sir, I don't know anything at all about it.

BARON: But I informed him myself that the Grand Duchess had had a child, the Grand Duchess of Saxe-Coburg-Gotha. Germain, this is no small affair.

GERMAIN: I can imagine.

BARON: I wrote him that Milord Desprez himself had come to see me the night before last. Milord Desprez came all the way from Saint-Cloud. He came to advise me that the Minister wished me to be in his office the next morning, that is to say, yesterday. I was going to carry out this order, when I learned that the Minister had gone to Versailles, to accompany the King. Accordingly I presented myself at Versailles. Since I knew what was involved, there was no time to lose, you understand.

GERMAIN: No doubt of it.

BARON: The Minister was out hunting. They directed me

      to see Milord de Gercourt, who led me in secret to
the private apartments, but—the King had just left
for Fontainebleau.

GERMAIN: How irritating.

BARON: Not at all. I mention it only to show you that I
am always punctual.

GERMAIN: Oh! No question of that.

BARON: In this world, punctuality is the best of all
virtues. You might even say it is the basis, the true
key to all the others. Because just as the most
beautiful aria in an opera, the most splendid piece of
eloquence, would be unpleasant at the wrong time or
place, just so the rarest virtues and the most gracious
manners are valuable only if you can produce them at
the exact and appropriate moment. Remember that,
Germain: nothing is more pathetic than arriving at
the wrong time, no matter what a splendid fellow you
are. Think of that celebrated diplomat, who arrived
too late at the deathbed of his monarch, and
found—the queen putting her hair in curlers. The
most sublimely gifted men can destroy themselves
that way. How many have we seen, covered with glory
in the army, or even in the cabinet, who've thrown it
all away for lack of a workable and regularly adjusted
watch! I trust yours is working well, my friend?

GERMAIN: I check it constantly, sir.

BARON: Excellent. To wind up, I should tell you that,
having met at Versailles the Marchioness of Morivaux,
who allowed me to ride in her carriage, I learned that I
had been misled by inaccurate information, and that
the Minister had gone back to Paris. His Excellency
received me there at two-thirty, and had the grace to
inform me himself that, as I was just telling you, the

Grand Duchess of Saxe-Coburg-Gotha has had a
child, and that the King has selected me and my
nephew to present his compliments to her there.

GERMAIN: In Gotha, sir?

BARON: In Gotha, on the Rhine. It is a great honor for
your master.

GERMAIN: Yes, sir; but he's gone out.

BARON: That's what I can't understand. Do you mean
he's still the same distracted blockhead as always?
Still forgets everything you tell him?

GERMAIN: You can't say it too often, sir. It's not that he
forgets, he's just always thinking of something else.

BARON: He must be out of here and on his way up the
Rhine tomorrow morning, without any hitches. And
you tell me he's made no arrangements whatever for
leaving?

GERMAIN: No, sir. Just this morning, before going out, he
did open up a large brassbound trunk, and he walked
round and round it for a good long time.

BARON: And did he put anything in the trunk?

GERMAIN: A sheet of music paper.

BARON: A sheet of music paper?

GERMAIN: Yes, sir; and then he closed the trunk, locked
it up very carefully, and put the key in his pocket.

BARON: A sheet of music paper! Always another lunacy! If
the King knew how sick the boy was, do you think he
would dare trust him with a mission of this
importance? A good thing I keep such a close eye on
him. Well, go on, what did he say, what did he do?

GERMAIN: He sang, sir. All day long.

BARON: He sang?

GERMAIN: Beautifully, sir. It was a pleasure to listen to
him.

BARON: A pretty start for an ambassador! Germain, you have a certain amount of good sense. Tell me, do you really think him capable of conducting himself rationally in a delicate situation like this?

GERMAIN: You mean going to Gotha, sir, and congratulating a mother on her newborn child? I imagine I could do it myself.

BARON: You don't know what you're talking about.

GERMAIN: Lord, sir, I'm talking about the Grand Duchess; you're the one who told me she just had a child.

BARON: It's true that she has just brought into the world the newest shoot of an ancient family tree. . . . But what can be keeping my nephew?

GERMAIN: He does come here, day in and day out, to call on the Countess.

BARON: And where might the Countess be?

GERMAIN: Sir, she hasn't gotten up yet.

BARON: At five P.M.! That's inconceivable. Doesn't the woman dine?

GERMAIN: No, sir; she sups.

BARON: Another scatterbrain! Is the whole neighborhood lunatic?

GERMAIN: My master would be very angry, sir, if he heard you talk that way. When anyone tries to point out to him the least sign of distraction on his part, he flies into a frightful rage. For instance, the other day he almost killed me because he had sprinkled snuff on his strawberries instead of sugar. And then again yesterday—

BARON: God of Justice! Can you believe that a man of quality, and of the very highest quality at that,

Germain—because my nephew is the soul of distinction—could fall into such a deplorable state!

GERMAIN: It's not a pretty picture, sir.

BARON: With my own eyes I've seen him, at the King's ball, saunter through the middle of a quadrille with his hands in his pockets, as if he were strolling in a garden.

GERMAIN: My word! Sir, he did the exact same thing the other night, here at the Countess's. It was a splendid party, and the local poet, Master Vertigo, recited a dramatic poem to music. At the most touching moment, sir, when the young girl who's been poisoned recognizes her father among her murderers, when all the women in the audience were collapsing in tears, my master gets up, strolls over to the author's table, and drinks the glass of water he has beside him. He ruined the whole effect of the scene.

BARON: That doesn't surprise me at all. One afternoon a charming young lady offered him a cup of tea, and he dropped thirty cents in it, under the impression she was collecting for the poor.

GERMAIN: Last winter, sir, you were away, around the time of his brother's marriage. Naturally, he had to play host at the wedding banquet. I came to his room that evening to help him dress. He sends me away, takes off his afternoon clothes, then paces up and down for nearly an hour—in his underwear, if you'll excuse the expression; then he comes to a sudden halt, and looks at himself in the mirror with complete astonishment: "What the hell am I doing?" he asks himself. "Good Lord, it's nighttime! I'm going to bed." Then he went and lay down on his bed, and would have forgotten all about the wedding and the dinner party if we hadn't come to remind him.

BARON: And you think a fantastic madman like this is capable of going to Gotha? Think how difficult my task is, Germain, because I must, whether I like it or not, carry out the King's orders. There's no question about it, because it's my nephew who has the title; I'm only accompanying him. He was given this title because he bears his father's name, which is greater than mine, and yet all the responsibility is on my shoulders.

GERMAIN: Since the distinction is my master's.

BARON: No doubt, but is that enough? He did promise me he would reform.

GERMAIN: He does try, sir, bit by bit; but he hates it when anyone contradicts him, and if you take my advice—but here he is.

MARQUIS *(Entering)*: There you are! What kind of game is this? Why do you always have to steal my papers?

GERMAIN: Sir, your uncle the Baron is here—

MARQUIS: Listen, clown, what did you do with the sheet of music paper I had this morning? Where did you put it? Where's it gone?

BARON: Good day, Valberg; what are you doing?

MARQUIS: Spring cleaning; one of these days I'll clean the whole lot of you out of here. *(To the Baron, who is laughing)* And you'll be the first, you bandit.

GERMAIN: Sir, it's the Baron.

MARQUIS: Oh, I'm sorry, Uncle, have you just come from Paris? I'm trying to find this sheet of music paper.

GERMAIN *(Softly to Baron)*: It must be the one he locked up so carefully.

BARON: You see how punctual I am, nephew, I've arrived exactly when I said I would. And are you all ready to go?

MARQUIS: To go?

BARON: Yes, tomorrow morning.

MARQUIS: Yes, on my honor; if the answer is no, I'll leave this minute and you'll never see me again as long as you live.

BARON: If what answer is no? What are you talking about?

MARQUIS: Yes, I swear to you, if I'm received coldly, if my declaration is not accepted, then for me the die is irrevocably cast.

BARON: But how could you be received coldly, or your declaration not accepted, since you come from the King?

MARQUIS: What business does the King have meddling in this affair?

BARON: Good Lord, it's obvious; you'll be carrying a letter personally signed by His Majesty.

MARQUIS: To the Countess?

BARON: To the Grand Duchess. Have you forgotten you have a diplomatic mission to carry out?

MARQUIS: I just got mixed up, because I also have a letter to write to the Countess. Have you seen her?

BARON: No, she's still asleep.

MARQUIS: Well, what do you think of the whole affair? Am I doing the right thing?

BARON: What whole affair?

MARQUIS: Oh, good heavens, I know what you're going to tell me: You should never have put up with it, you've gotten entangled with her, you've given her grounds for a lawsuit; now, I ask you, what's the good of all that? So you had your lawyer spout a lot of words over a vineyard that wasn't worth fighting for; now he's in parliament. His speeches make no sense at all. I know, I know, that's politics, but it has nothing to do with the case, and you'll see, his bill will be voted down.

BARON: What *are* you jabbering about? We've got something serious to deal with here, that requires all your attention.

MARQUIS: If that's not how things are, just say so. Speak, sir, I'm all ears.

BARON: This is about our service as ambassadors. Did you read the memorandum I sent you?

MARQUIS: Our service as ambassadors? Yes, of course; I'm always ready to serve the King.

BARON: I'm glad to hear it.

MARQUIS: His Majesty knows my devotion.

BARON: Marvelous. Then you will be ready—

MARQUIS: How can you doubt it? I've given my orders; Germain, is everything ready?

GERMAIN: Sir, I haven't had any orders at all.

MARQUIS: What? You joker! What about the huge trunk I had you put in my room?

GERMAIN: Oh, sir, if you're planning to sing along the way . . .

MARQUIS: Sing? You impertinent fool, what do you mean?

GERMAIN: Oh, sir, your music is in the trunk, and the key is in your pocket.

MARQUIS: In my. . . . Oh! Good grief, it's true. They must have given it to me with my gloves and handkerchief when I went out. These bumpkins never notice anything.

GERMAIN: I can assure you, sir—

BARON: Not another word, leave us, and go get everything ready.

Exit Germain.

Now Valberg, I must leave you, to take these letters from the court to Milord Duplessis. I've only one thing to tell you: keep in mind that our trip is no ordinary mission, and that your whole future may depend on the amount of skill you display.

MARQUIS: Alas! I'm all too well aware of it.

BARON: That's why you must promise me you'll make a real effort to keep yourself in order, so you can conduct your affairs intelligently, and get over these little distractions, these mental lapses which are always so embarrassing.

MARQUIS: Oh, I promise you, that's over.

BARON: Are you serious?

MARQUIS: A hundred percent serious.

BARON: Then go finish giving your orders for the trip. It's now five-forty; I'll go back over to see Milord Duplessis, it's not far, I'll be back by dinnertime. So, do you promise to take my advice at every step? You know what these court gentlemen are like.

MARQUIS: Oh, have no fear. I know how to behave with them. Just let me get these instructions written out. Wait, though, I need to know the name of your attorney; I'll see him myself.

BARON: My attorney? I don't have an attorney. What are you talking about?

MARQUIS: Oh, if you're not represented in the case, then I should talk directly to the judge.

BARON: Judge? What judge? About what?

MARQUIS: About your court case.

BARON: But I don't have a court case.

MARQUIS: What! Didn't you just say I had to go speak to the court?

BARON: I was speaking of the royal court of Saxe-Coburg-Gotha.

MARQUIS: Oh! Yes, of course, our diplomatic mission. . . . I've been a little preoccupied; it's the Countess who has a court case going on, and she's begged me to keep an eye on it. What a charming woman!

BARON: Yes, yes, we know you're mad about her, and you bury yourself in this out-of-the-way place only because her house is up here. But you must not let this inclination of yours get in the way of our plans, please.

MARQUIS: Never fear, go on your way, don't worry. When I'm not paying attention, you see, I seem very casual about everything, but when I'm involved in important affairs, nobody's more attentive and alert.

BARON: All in good time.

MARQUIS: Go to Milord Duplessis, don't worry, I'll take care of everything else.

BARON: We'll see how precisely you do it.

MARQUIS: I'll keep a careful eye on Germain, to make sure he doesn't make any foolish mistakes.

BARON: Very good.

MARQUIS: I'll finish getting all my papers in order. I've got quite a lot of them.

BARON: Don't get me behind schedule, I beg you.

MARQUIS: Heaven forbid! Go on, sir, deliver His Majesty's letters; I've got to write to my mother—I should write and thank the Minister too; I'll leave my dogs with Madame de Belleclaire, I'll let our family know about our trip, and I hope by the time you get back, the marriage contract will be settled.

BARON *(Stopping just as he was about to leave)*: Marriage contract! What marriage contract?

MARQUIS: Why, mine, of course; didn't you know?

BARON: What kind of joke is this? Did you say your marriage?

MARQUIS: Yes, to the Countess; didn't I tell you we were getting married?

BARON: Not really. This is quite a piece of news.

MARQUIS: It's given me a lot to do, as you can see.

BARON: But people don't get married the day before they go off on a trip. These arrangements are for when you get back.

MARQUIS: Not at all; my fate will be settled today.

BARON: My friend, you can't mean that seriously.

MARQUIS: I mean it very seriously, because I'm not leaving until I get the right answer from her.

BARON: But what does it have to do with our diplomatic mission whether her answer is right or wrong? I assume you don't plan to bring the Countess with you?

MARQUIS: Why not, if she says yes?

BARON: Lord have mercy, a woman on a trip? Hats, dresses, chambermaids, a blizzard of parcels, stopping every night at an inn, incessant pleading for a closed carriage!

MARQUIS: What you're talking about is all trivial.

BARON: What I'm talking about is our appearance there, which is not trivial at all. The letters I carry do not have one word in them about your being accompanied by a wife, and I don't know if it would be thought proper.

MARQUIS: That is less important to me than anything.

BARON: But it is extremely important to me, that's what I'm trying to tell you, and if you persist in this, I swear to you—

The Marquis has gone over to the piano, where he strums a few chords as if about to play something.

Really, the boy is mad; he can't possibly go to Gotha. What can I do? I can't very well go by myself; his name is all over the King's letters. If I tell the Minister what's really going on, there'll be a scandal, and even if I arrange for my name to be put in place of his—which would be only fair—it would mean a considerable delay, and the whole trip would become pointless.

We hear someone ringing for a servant.

Good Lord! That's the Countess ringing—I'll miss Milord Duplessis. Nephew, listen to me, for heaven's sake.

MARQUIS: Sir, I thought you'd gone.

BARON: You are in love with the Countess.

MARQUIS: That's my secret.

BARON: But you just confided it to me.

MARQUIS: Well, since it slipped out, I won't hide it any longer.

BARON: No more of these jokes, I beg you. I cannot speak to the Countess on your behalf; she loathes the sight of me, and besides I'm in a hurry. Here's what I propose: we have two matters to see through to a happy ending, your marriage and your royal mission. We can't sacrifice either of them to the other.

MARQUIS: That's all I ask in the world.

BARON: Go see the Countess, get an answer from her. If she agrees to marry you, I won't object to her coming to Germany with us, though it would mean putting our trip off till the day after tomorrow, of course.

MARQUIS: Of course.

BARON: Or she might always join us there later.

MARQUIS: Now that is a really excellent idea.

BARON: Don't you think so? And then if she turns you down—

MARQUIS: If she turns me down, I'll leave her forever.

BARON: Exactly; we always fly from ingratitude.

MARQUIS: Oh, but I'll always adore her!

BARON: Of course. *(Aside)* He's not really a bad boy; even these deranged spells of his could turn out well for him, if properly handled. Till now I just didn't know how to guide him. Now, he's ready to go to Gotha. *(To Marquis)* Well, then, it's all arranged, so I'll leave you. When I get back, your fate will be decided— favorably, I assume, since the Countess is apparently just waiting for you to propose.

MARQUIS: Favorably? I'm not so sure. You see, I've come here so many times to propose to her, and—I don't know how it happens, but somehow I always forget. But this time I've made sure; I put a note in my snuffbox to remind me.

BARON: It will certainly be a very modern marriage.

MARQUIS: I still don't know if she'll say yes, because it's very hard to keep her mind on one subject for a long time. When you talk to her, she seems to be listening, but she's really a million miles away.

BARON: Perhaps she's a little deranged too?

MARQUIS: Yes, exactly, she's deranged; it's intolerable.

BARON: Oh, talk about the pot calling the kettle—well, I must go to Milord Duplessis.

MARQUIS: Yes, do that, because this marriage, the Countess's court case, our diplomatic mission—it all has me totally preoccupied. I've got a thousand letters to answer, there's a new novel she wants me to read— I can't possibly do it all at once—you know how these things are.

BARON: Yes, yes, keep your mind on your marriage.

MARQUIS: That's right, all these diplomatic affairs get me horribly confused. I just won't think about them. Let me show you out.

BARON: What? Oh, no, no. I'll leave you to your own devices. *(Aside, as he goes out)* He said he'd keep an eye on Germain, but I think I'd better have Germain keep an eye on him!

MARQUIS: Ho there! Servants!

VICTORIA *(Entering)*: What would you like, sir?

MARQUIS: Bring me my dressing gown.

VICTORIA: Oh, sir, you must be joking.

MARQUIS: Joking! Oh! . . . yes, of course.

VICTORIA: The Countess has been told that you're here, and she'll be right with you.

MARQUIS: But why? Just let me get my hair arranged, and I'll go right over to her house.

VICTORIA: But, sir, you *are* at her house.

MARQUIS: Oh, you're right . . . what I meant was . . .

VICTORIA: Here's the Countess now, sir.

COUNTESS *(Entering; over her shoulder)*: François, send Victoria to me.

VICTORIA: Here I am, madame.

COUNTESS: Oh, good. *(To Marquis)* Milord de Valberg,

I'm so pleased to see you. You were so delightfully entertaining yesterday. . . . I'm wild about you when you carry on like that.

MARQUIS: That's no way to improve my behavior, madame; on the other hand, they do say two extremes meet in the middle.

COUNTESS: Victoria, I must have my gown.

VICTORIA: Yes, madame.

COUNTESS: And get me another collar. *(She sits at her dressing table)* This one's simply horrible. *(To Marquis)* Do sit down.

VICTORIA: But, madame, you can merely take the collar off if you don't like it; it's a very nice one, too. There's just a little crease here. . . . Allow me. *(She rearranges the Countess's collar)*

COUNTESS: Yes, a crease, you see.

She watches in the mirror as Victoria fixes her collar.

Yes, that's just what I meant. Now it looks marvelous. Have Mademoiselle Dufour make me another one just like it, but I mean exactly, you understand.

VICTORIA: Yes, madame. And when would you want it?

COUNTESS: When? Why, tomorrow morning, of course. You can simply have François go over and get it first thing, I'll need it right then.

VICTORIA: But madame, there may not be enough time.

COUNTESS: Oh, of course! When I want something, you always decide it's impossible. And then you come and tell me how fond of me you are.

VICTORIA: But I truly am—Madame is very unfair.

COUNTESS: All right, all right, get me some rouge. Well, Milord Valberg, you haven't said a word.

MARQUIS: But, madame, you've been talking to someone else.

COUNTESS: You're right, you're right, forgive me. Now what was it you were saying? Something about extremes?

MARQUIS: Extremes? No, I think . . . could it have been dreams?

COUNTESS: That might have been it. Victoria!

VICTORIA: Madame?

COUNTESS: But I don't remember what it was I wanted to say about your dreams.

MARQUIS: Oh, give me a moment, and I'll tell you all about them.

COUNTESS: With pleasure. I love listening to you.

MARQUIS: Will you have a great many guests today?

COUNTESS: Not if you don't want me to. I was just going to ask you about that, because everyone who gets bored in town seems to think my park is their promenade. Victoria! See that no callers are admitted.

VICTORIA: I was just going to suggest that, madame.

MARQUIS: I'm very grateful, because I've got something quite serious to talk to you about.

COUNTESS *(To Victoria)*: Oh, except for my sister-in-law, of course.

VICTORIA: Yes, madame.

COUNTESS: She's mad about you, you know, Milord Valberg.

MARQUIS: Well, I find her charming too. There are some women, like her, who simply seduce you the moment you lay eyes on them.

COUNTESS: Oh, and Victoria, tell them to make sure to let Milord de Clervaut in.

VICTORIA: Is that all?

MARQUIS: Oh, madame, Milord de Latour also, if you don't mind.

COUNTESS: Milord de Latour? Oh, very well, Milord de Latour too; I don't mind.

VICTORIA: I'll go tell the gatekeeper.

COUNTESS: Wait—the people who were here yesterday too.

VICTORIA: But yesterday Madame had open house, and everyone came.

COUNTESS: Are you sure?

VICTORIA: Absolutely.

COUNTESS: Oh, well, in that case, let everyone in.

VICTORIA: Does Madame have any further need of me?

COUNTESS: No, no—however, stay nearby—and make sure they let me know as soon as the new fabrics get here.

Victoria goes out.

MARQUIS: Have you been shopping?

COUNTESS: Yes, for winter clothes.

MARQUIS: You love being worldly, madame.

COUNTESS: No doubt; it's all I know how to do. You know how unhappy my late husband made me, those three years he kept me in isolation with him on his estate.

MARQUIS: On his estate?

COUNTESS: Yes, so very far out in the country, three years without a break—except when we took that trip up the Rhine.

MARQUIS: You traveled up the Rhine?

COUNTESS: Yes, all the way up to Gotha.

MARQUIS: Is the countryside beautiful there?

COUNTESS: I really couldn't tell you. It takes so much effort to get from one place to the next, and they all look the same to me. I simply can't tell the difference. They showed me castles, forests, rivers, churches, especially churches. . . . Oh, God, those Gothic churches are so cold! You catch a chill you think won't ever leave you. I can still remember waking up in a nice warm bed, all bruised and shaken from the coach trip the night before, and my husband walking into the room to propose that we see yet another Gothic cathedral!

MARQUIS: Yes, that must have been very painful.

COUNTESS: Being locked up in a Turkish harem would have been more pleasant. And bear in mind that it wasn't enough for him just to drag me through those dank caverns, so I could throw my neck out trying to get a good look at the rose windows. No, my husband had to climb up into the roof-beams, hauling me along after him; that was his triumph. Do you know what an effort that is? You clamber up around a dusty old column, in a little tower where the air is suffocating, and you keep going up and around, up and around, till you feel like there's a corkscrew going into your brain, till you start to get seasick from the motion, all the while keeping your eyes closed so you won't look down and fall. And that's just the moment when your guide takes a little spyglass from his pocket and invites you to admire the view. And that's how I saw Germany.

MARQUIS: I suppose that's the same route we'll be taking with the Baron.

COUNTESS: What, is the Baron here?

MARQUIS: Yes, madame, he's just arrived. He came from

Paris this morning, during that big rainstorm—I suppose that's why the weather's so terrible.

COUNTESS *(Laughing)*: Why, because the Baron's here? Oh, you're too funny!

MARQUIS: I'm sorry, weren't we talking about the Baron?

COUNTESS *(Laughing)*: Of course, of course! Oh, you're marvelous.

MARQUIS: That's what I thought. I know I get confused sometimes, and I can't abide that.

COUNTESS: Oh, no—when that happens I always find you adorable. *(She is looking for something)*

MARQUIS: What are you looking for? Some snuff? I've got a very good mixture. *(He opens his snuffbox)* Oh! I completely forgot!

COUNTESS: What?

MARQUIS: You see that piece of paper in there? Guess what it says.

COUNTESS: I can't guess, just tell me.

MARQUIS: It's to remind me to ask you if you intend to marry again.

COUNTESS *(Now searching at the piano)*: Well?

MARQUIS: What is it you keep looking for?

COUNTESS: Go on talking, don't mind me.

MARQUIS: You'd be the happiest woman in the world if you married me.

COUNTESS *(Still searching)*: If I married you?

MARQUIS: Yes, of course.

COUNTESS: I can't see it. It's unimaginable!

MARQUIS: Exactly what is it you're looking for?

COUNTESS: A sheet of paper; I had it a minute ago.

MARQUIS: Is it very important?

COUNTESS: Yes and no; it's a song.

MARQUIS: I've got a good collection. I'll lend it to you if

you like. It's fairly complete from 1650 on.

COUNTESS: It was a new song.

MARQUIS: I've got a great many of them.

COUNTESS: New songs?

MARQUIS: Well, new for their time.

COUNTESS *(Laughing)*: Oh, yes, for 1650! Ha, ha, ha! You're incorrigible.

MARQUIS: Well, I don't change. But as you know, being consistent isn't always the way to succeed with women.

COUNTESS: You have complaints about the way women treat you?

MARQUIS: Oh! If only you wanted to be mine—someone's coming.

COUNTESS: It's your valet.

GERMAIN *(Entering)*: Pardon me, madame. I have a message for Milord from the Baron.

MARQUIS: Oh, good grief, it must be— *(Taking papers)* Oh! Oh, madame, this is truly amazing; what an adventure. Is this what you happen to be looking for?

COUNTESS: Heavens, I do believe that's it. Apparently you stole it from me. *(She puts the music—for that is what it is—on the piano, and plays)*

GERMAIN *(Aside)*: Quite right; I got it from his trunk. *(To the Marquis)* Sir, the Baron instructed me to ask you—

MARQUIS: What? What is it?

GERMAIN: If you were keeping your mind on your affairs.

MARQUIS: What! You come and disturb us for such a—

GERMAIN: It's because the Baron has just gotten an urgent letter from Fontainebleau, and it has him very worried. He's gone back to Milord Duplessis's house; he seems completely staggered.

MARQUIS: Really?

GERMAIN: Yes, and I brought this music just to have an

excuse for coming in, so I could warn you that he
must have an answer immediately.

MARQUIS *(Thinking it over)*: You did well. But it seems to
me— *(Going over to the piano)* That isn't it, madame,
you're mistaken; that's something else.

COUNTESS: But I recognized it immediately. Listen . . .
(She plays)

GERMAIN: It doesn't seem to me that they're discussing
their affairs. The Baron told me to overhear what I
could of their conversation. *(He begins to go out slowly,
while eavesdropping)*

COUNTESS: You see, that's how it's written.

MARQUIS: Oh, the music, yes. But as for the words . . .

COUNTESS: Oh, I don't know the words at all.

MARQUIS: Oh! Well, they go something like . . . *(Sings)*
"Sweetheart, the happy man who's at your side . . . "

GERMAIN *(Nearing the door)*: This won't get them on the
road to Gotha.

MARQUIS: That's strange; I can't remember the rest.

COUNTESS: Very strange, given your memory!

MARQUIS: Yes, normally I remember everything.

VICTORIA *(Entering)*: Madame, your fabrics have arrived.

COUNTESS: Oh, good.

MARQUIS: Do you have things to do? I don't mean to
monopolize your time.

COUNTESS: Won't you come look at them with me? You
can help me decide.

MARQUIS: No, I'm not going out today. I must stay here
and wait for someone I've got to talk to.

COUNTESS: Here? In my house?

MARQUIS: Yes—oh, well, now that I think of it—it's you.

COUNTESS: Me?

MARQUIS: Yes, haven't I told you?

COUNTESS: What?

MARQUIS: That I have an incredibly deep desire to marry you.

COUNTESS: I don't recall your saying so.

MARQUIS: Just a minute ago. That's what I came here for.

COUNTESS: I never noticed.

MARQUIS: But how could you have missed it? It's unbelievable to me how easily you get distracted. Anyway, I'm sure that—

COUNTESS: That what?

MARQUIS: That I told you all about my trip.

COUNTESS: What trip?

MARQUIS: Up the Rhine, to Gotha.

COUNTESS: What? No, that was me telling you all about mine.

MARQUIS: What do you mean, yours?

COUNTESS: The trip I took up the Rhine, with my late husband.

MARQUIS: I beg your pardon; I don't know what I was—

COUNTESS: You're wandering; come look at my fabrics. I'll give you my copy of those poems, by whatever-his-name-is, so you can find out how our little romanza ends.

MARQUIS: But I was the one who—

COUNTESS: No, I tell you, it was my trip.

They have left the room.

GERMAIN: Well, Miss Victoria, what do you make of all this? You know that Milord loves Madame.

VICTORIA: And I know that Madame loves Milord.

GERMAIN: And that Milord wants to marry Madame.

VICTORIA: And that Madame would like nothing better.

GERMAIN: Are you sure of that?

VICTORIA: Perfectly.

GERMAIN: But you may not be aware that we're going on a diplomatic mission.

VICTORIA: Oh?

GERMAIN: To Gotha. I gather from what I've been told that the Grand Duchess has just had a child, and we've been chosen to convey His Majesty's compliments to her.

VICTORIA: And what does that mean?

GERMAIN: It means that my master wants the Countess to tell him yes or no before he leaves, so his mind will be at rest. It means that we are leaving tomorrow morning with the Baron, that one word will settle the matter, and that instead of saying anything, my master and your mistress prefer to sing.

VICTORIA: But he did mention marriage and traveling, didn't he?

GERMAIN: And she answered by talking about songs.

VICTORIA: Why doesn't your Baron try to help them out?

GERMAIN: He's afraid that he'd ruin everything, because he's on bad terms with your mistress, or so he thinks.

VICTORIA: Milord Germain . . .

GERMAIN: Miss Victoria . . .

VICTORIA: Our employers are grown-up babies; it's up to us to get this affair settled. You just brought him a piece of music paper; isn't that what they were singing from?

GERMAIN: Yes, it's over there.

VICTORIA: Give it to me; and now . . . *(She writes on the songsheet)*

GERMAIN: What are you writing on it?

VICTORIA: Don't worry. Now, let's leave it on the piano.

GERMAIN *(Reading it)*: But what if they get angry?

VICTORIA: How could they? She dreams about him the whole day long. All the more reason—

GERMAIN: Here they come; let's go.

VICTORIA: And let's listen in.

Enter Countess and Marquis; he holds a book.

COUNTESS: You didn't like that pink peau-de-soie?

MARQUIS: No, it's not what I would choose. *(Reading)*
"Sweetheart, the happy man who's at your side . . . "

COUNTESS: You see how happy you are? Now that you have the book, you don't need to worry about your memory.

MARQUIS: Oh, good Lord, all I have to do is glance at it, and the whole thing comes back. *(Reading)*
"Sweetheart, the happy man who's at your side
Has met the stars and seen the heavens smile;
Your tender blushes, and your glance bright-eyed . . . "

COUNTESS: You put such feeling into it!

MARQUIS: Oh, madame, it's not difficult to put feeling into words that seem to come from the bottom of your heart. Don't these lines seem to have been written just so I could say them to you?
"Sweetheart, the happy man—"

COUNTESS: I think this is some game of yours.

MARQUIS: No, I swear to you on my soul, by everything that's holy in the world, I—I find these verses very charming.

COUNTESS: Well, then come and sing them; I'll accompany you. *(She sits at the piano)*

MARQUIS *(Sitting next to her)*: You'll see, I can do it

without the book. . . . But what are you thinking about now, madame?

COUNTESS: That pink peau-de-soie. You really didn't like it?

MARQUIS: No, I preferred that beige taffeta, like autumn leaves.

COUNTESS: But the fabric is too old.

MARQUIS: It looked brand-new to me.

COUNTESS: Never mind! Some things just always make you think of last year.

MARQUIS: What a thing to say; so typically feminine!

COUNTESS: What do you mean, feminine?

MARQUIS: Oh, you know, always wanting something new—that's how you women are.

COUNTESS: "You women!" How very polite.

MARQUIS: But you live for the present, and never think beyond that. You have no regard for what happened last night, and as for tomorrow, you never give it a moment's thought. I may say, if I were married, my wife wouldn't spend so much of her time daydreaming.

COUNTESS: And you'd make her wear a beige autumn-leaf dress?

MARQUIS: Yes, why not, if it suited my taste?

COUNTESS: She'd laugh at you and refuse to wear it.

MARQUIS: She'd wear it all her life, madame, if she really loved me.

COUNTESS: Well! On that basis, you'll stay a bachelor.

MARQUIS: Madame, are you serious?

COUNTESS: Yes, I advise you to give up your search for a willing victim.

MARQUIS: Oh, God! What you've just said is my death!

COUNTESS: What do you mean, your death?

MARQUIS: There's no question about it. I'm not like you,

madame. You don't have to tell *me* anything twice.
Oh! I was afraid you'd have harsh words for me, but I
never dreamed it would be like this. It horrifies me, it
drives me to despair. . . . Oh, God in heaven! Don't
say it again.

COUNTESS: But, good Lord, what's gotten into you?

MARQUIS: Do you think I can go on in this world without
you near me, without everything I hold dear? My life
would be unbearable. Laugh as much as you like,
madame. I know you'll tell me that traveling in haste
is always a bore, that you have obligations and things
to do just as I have. What am I saying? That you'll
find a hundred excuses, raise a hundred difficulties—
but would you notice a single one of them if you
loved me? Is it your court case that keeps you here?
I've already told you that it's been settled in your
favor. I had to go see your lawyer twenty times. He
lives a long way from here, but what does that matter
to you? It doesn't bother you at all—no, madame,
because you don't love me. And if I ever—

COUNTESS: I hate to interrupt you, but what is this
gigantic rigamarole all about?

MARQUIS: Every word I'm saying is the exact truth; but
since you don't wish to hear it, I'll leave. Adieu,
madame.

COUNTESS: Do you know something, Marquis? These
little spells of madness you have are only tolerable
when they're amusing. No one would dream of
getting angry at you when you walk off wearing your
neighbor's hat, or you say, "Good morning, miss," to
the village priest. But you shouldn't let that encourage
you to lose your mind entirely, and talk as if you're
going to drown yourself over a dress in autumn-leaf

beige. Because you have to understand, just between us, that when that happens it's no longer fun for everyone else; you're trying our patience, and that's never a good idea, especially with women.

MARQUIS: That must mean I've been getting too insistent. All the more reason for me to leave you for good.

COUNTESS: You have really lost your wits.

MARQUIS: Better and better—oh, I'm so unhappy!

COUNTESS: You won't have supper with me?

MARQUIS: No, I'm leaving.—Farewell, madame! *(He sits in a corner of the room)*

COUNTESS: Really, do whatever you want; you are both unbearable and incomprehensible. Go on, leave me to my music. What's this? *(She has gone back to the piano, and softly reads what is written on the music sheet)*

MARQUIS *(Sitting)*: And I loved her so tenderly! How could I have upset her this way! What did I do to get her so offended? What! I come here, my heart full of love for her, to lay my whole life at her feet; I declare my love confidently, in all sincerity; I ask for her hand as clearly and straightforwardly as I can; and she rejects me brutally! It's unimaginable; the more I think about it, the less I understand it. *(He gets up and paces around the room in great strides, not noticing the Countess)* It must be that I've committed some inexcusable lapse without realizing it.

COUNTESS *(Trying to hand him the paper as he passes by)*: Here, Valberg, read this.

MARQUIS *(As before)*: But it can't be! What inexcusable thing could I have done? When I come to see her again, she'll forgive me. Come on, Germain, I want to go now. Yes, definitely, I must see her again. She's so good, so understanding! And so kind and so beautiful! No woman in the world can compare to her.

COUNTESS *(Aside)*: I'll wait till this little spell of madness is over.

MARQUIS *(As before)*: Of course, it's true that she's a devilish flirt, and lazy—hopelessly lazy! And she continually says the silliest things—

COUNTESS *(Offering him the paper)*: Terribly inaccurate likeness, Milord Valberg!

MARQUIS *(As before)*: And if a woman continually says the silliest things, how could she really suit a reasonable man like me? Would she have the calm, the presence of mind, the reliability you need to run a household? —A woman like her would need to be kept in line.

COUNTESS: This is worth hearing.

MARQUIS: But then she's such a good musician! Germain! Oh, we would be so happy alone, in some peaceful little retreat, with just a few friends to visit, and everything she loves around us—because if she loves something, I would be sure to love it, too.

COUNTESS: All in good time.

MARQUIS: But no, she loves society, parties, crowds!— Germain!—Well, so what! I wouldn't be jealous. Who could be, with such a wife?—Germain!—I'd leave her to do as she pleased; for her sake, I'd love things that bore me to tears; I'd be proud when other men admired her; I'd treat her with the same dignity I grant myself; and if she ever betrayed me—Germain! —I'd plunge a dagger into her heart.

COUNTESS *(Catching his upraised hand)*: Oh, no, Milord de Valberg!

MARQUIS: Countess, it's you! Good God! I didn't realize—

COUNTESS: Before you kill me, read this.

MARQUIS *(Taking paper)*: Now what's this? *(Reading)* "We beg Milord Marquis not to forget that he must marry the Countess before leaving for Germany." Well! You see, madame, that was me and not you talking about that trip.

COUNTESS: But is that true, are you leaving?

MARQUIS: How can you ask! I've been going mad telling you over and over for the last two hours.

COUNTESS: You must have confused me with my chambermaid, because this note is in her handwriting.

MARQUIS: Really? She writes quite well.

COUNTESS: Perhaps, but she has no business writing such stuff.

MARQUIS: On the contrary, this is just what I was thinking.

COUNTESS: But what are you going to do in Germany?

MARQUIS: Convey His Majesty's compliments to the Grand Duchess of Gotha.

COUNTESS: And when do you leave?

MARQUIS: Tomorrow morning.

COUNTESS: Were you planning to marry me en route, in the carriage perhaps?

MARQUIS: Certainly. I wanted to take you with me. It would be the most delightful trip!

COUNTESS: Is this an elopement?

MARQUIS: Well, strictly speaking—

COUNTESS: They're always so romantic.

MARQUIS: Of course, we would publish the banns—

COUNTESS: Whenever we changed horses, I suppose. And the witnesses?

MARQUIS: We have my uncle.

COUNTESS: What about your parents?

MARQUIS: They couldn't ask for a better match.

COUNTESS: And the world?

MARQUIS: What can the world say? We're perfectly decent people, I expect. They won't think we're bankrupts escaping their debtors, just because we go off in a carriage together.

COUNTESS: Your plan is so absurd, and so extravagant, that I find it truly amusing.

MARQUIS: Just follow it, and everything will be simple.

COUNTESS: I'm almost tempted.

MARQUIS: I'm entranced. Ho! Germain!

GERMAIN *(Entering)*: Did you call, sir? *(Aside)* I think we're out of the woods now.

MARQUIS: Quick, go and get that big brassbound trunk that's in the middle of my room at home, and bring it here as fast as you can.

GERMAIN: Here, sir?

MARQUIS: Yes, and hurry!

Germain goes out.

COUNTESS *(Laughing)*: Good God, what lunacy! You sent him to get your trunk?

MARQUIS: Yes, we've got to start packing immediately. You know, when you get a good idea, you must act on it first thing; that's what I've been taught.

COUNTESS: Just a second, Marquis; before we go careening off at top speed to the East Indies, we must get our papers in order. Are you convinced that I've been blessed with all the necessary qualities to manage one of your towering castles in Spain?

MARQUIS: Castles in Spain? I don't know what you're talking about.

COUNTESS: Do I possess the calm, the presence of mind,

the steadiness you need to run a household, especially when the master sets such a shining example?

MARQUIS: You're making fun of me. Do I really have to tell you again what the whole world knows, that you have all the qualities, all the talents, and all the graces on earth?

COUNTESS: But you forget that I'm a devilish flirt, and hopelessly lazy, and silly, oh, yes, I continually say the silliest things.

MARQUIS: Madame, who ever said anything like that?

COUNTESS: Oh, a friend of mine.

MARQUIS: An impertinent creature.

COUNTESS: Not always. He's quite an original character; he does portraits of others before his mirror, and paints them all in his own image. Can you guess his name? He's a diplomat and a fairly good musician, a poet who's a connoisseur of fabrics, a huntsman quite dangerous to his neighbor's hedges, and when playing cards a formidable opponent—to his partner. He's a wit who says idiotic things, and a true gentleman who sometimes does them; to sum up, he's a lover so sensitive that, to win a woman's heart, he pays her pro forma compliments when he's attentive, and insults her when he's distracted.

MARQUIS: If I've done such things, madame, I swear I shall never do them again, and you'll see on this trip—

COUNTESS: Have I said I'm going with you on this trip?

MARQUIS: You did say yes.

COUNTESS: I almost said yes, but there is a whole world between "yes" and "almost."

MARQUIS: But do say yes, madame, and this portrait you've just drawn will no longer resemble me. And I must add in protest, if it does look like me now, it's all thanks to you. The state I've been in, of incessant doubt, fear, hope, uncertainty, has kept me from seeing and hearing, from understanding anything that wasn't you. Don't insult me by thinking that I would have lost my wits even if I didn't love you so much; the truth is I left them in your hands; it will only take one word from you to restore them.

COUNTESS: What you've just said gives me a very amusing notion: it could be that, without our realizing it, we simply stole each other's wits away. You've been going out of your mind, you say, with love of me; perhaps I've been so continually silly because of my fondness for you. Tell me, Marquis, should we try to repair the damage we've done to each other? Since I've taken your good sense, as you have mine, why don't we simply take each other's good advice? Perhaps that way we could arrive at a superb mutual understanding.

MARQUIS: I ask nothing better than to obey you.

COUNTESS: It's not a question of obeying, but of a fair exchange. For instance, you've told me that I'm lazy—

MARQUIS: But, madame—

COUNTESS: You've told me so, and I believe you. You, in contrast, are always restless; you come back from hunting when I'm just getting up; I loathe the thought of writing anything, while your fingers are incessantly stained with ink. It's exactly the same with reading: you devour tragedies ferociously, act by act, while the gentle hum of their oratory sends me right to sleep. On the other hand, in society you're at a total loss, like the legendary courtier who hung his periwig on the candelabra: you don't say a word, or else you talk to yourself, without noticing anyone around you;

whereas I, and I have to admit it, love to chatter, even
to gossip if there's not too many people around, and
while you're off in a corner, sulking, with a fierce look
on your face, the noise diverts me, carries me away; a
dance sweeps me off my feet. Couldn't we put all
these contrasts into a formal tableau? Find a
framework in which we could put your autumn-leaf
beige next to my pink peau-de-soie, our virtues side
by side with our defects, where we could take turns
being the blind man and the seeing-eye dog. Wouldn't
that be a lovely example to set before the world, a
marriage in which the man was deep enough in love
to give up saying, "I want," and the woman would
give up even more—the pleasure of saying, "If I
wanted"?

MARQUIS: You enchant me, you send me reeling. Oh,
madame! If you thought me worthy to turn my entire
life over to you, I would die of joy at your feet.

COUNTESS: Oh, no; then what good would your life do
me?

GERMAIN *(Coming in with the trunk)*: Here's your trunk,
sir.

MARQUIS: And my uncle?

GERMAIN: He hasn't come back from seeing Milord
Duplessis.

MARQUIS: Well, madame?

COUNTESS: Well . . . let's try.

MARQUIS: Quick, Germain, François, Victoria, bring
everyone in here.

COUNTESS: Is this the way you thank me for accepting
you?

MARQUIS: Oh, madame! I'll have plenty of time to do that.

COUNTESS: Plenty of time? The things you say!

MARQUIS: Of course I will, because from this day on, that's all I want to do for the rest of my life.

VICTORIA *(Entering)*: Does Madame need me?

COUNTESS: You're the one, Miss Victoria, who took the liberty of—

MARQUIS: Don't scold her. If I had the crown diamonds in my hand now, instead of throwing them out the window, I'd put them in her pocket.

He gives Victoria a purse of money.

COUNTESS: So much for having your wits restored!

MARQUIS: Oh, madame! We're allowed one day of indulgence. First of all, bring out all your music.

COUNTESS: Here's a good beginning.

MARQUIS *(Sorting through the music)*: The Germans are very fond of music. We'll find connoisseurs there. I'll give a soiree so I can watch you sing for them. *(Sings)*

"Sweetheart, the happy man who . . . "

Those German nobles will adore you. Germain!

GERMAIN: Sir?

MARQUIS: Get me my violin.

Germain goes out.

COUNTESS: Make sure you pack that song, at least.

MARQUIS: It'll always remind me of the happiest day of my life.

COUNTESS: And my beige autumn-leaf gown? Victoria!

VICTORIA: Yes, madame.

She brings the dress; an instant later Germain appears with the violin.

MARQUIS: Then you will wear it?

COUNTESS: Since that's one of your conditions.

MARQUIS: Oh, good Lord! Not if it makes you unhappy! Miss Victoria, bring some other dresses. *(He throws the beige gown over a piece of furniture)*

COUNTESS: Do you know what we should do? Pack very little, only the essentials; we can buy all sorts of things while we're there.

MARQUIS: That's absolutely right. Germain!

GERMAIN: Sir?

MARQUIS: Bring only my rifle and my hunting horn; yes, we'll buy everything else in Gotha.

COUNTESS: Gotha?

MARQUIS: Of course, that's where we're going.

COUNTESS: Oh! Here, take this little chest.

MARQUIS: What's in it, your family papers? *(Opening it)* Oh, it's tea; but you can find that anywhere.

COUNTESS: Ah, but this is the only kind I can tolerate.

MARQUIS: Oh, we're going to have such a lovely time!

COUNTESS: We can buy some German outfits there; they'll be wonderful for a masquerade when we get home.

MARQUIS: Madame, why don't we take my sundial? It keeps perfect time.

COUNTESS: Are you mad, Valberg? After all your promises?

MARQUIS: You're right; my pocket watch will do. *(He puts it into the trunk)*

COUNTESS: Remember, we must keep a careful eye on you, now that you're a diplomat.

MARQUIS: Oh, don't worry, I've been well trained. *(He takes various objects at random from the room, and puts them into the trunk. Talking all the while, he also puts in*

his portfolio, his gloves, his handkerchief, and his hat) I've
already served in Denmark, where I did very well. My
uncle, who thinks he knows everything, tried to show
me what to do, but his mind isn't really all there; just
between us, he's a little bit dotty! *(Closes the trunk)*

COUNTESS: And here he is.

BARON *(Entering)*: Madame, I beg your pardon for coming
in so abruptly, without being announced, but some
unforeseen circumstances—

COUNTESS: It's a great pleasure to see you, sir.

MARQUIS: Oh, kiss me, dear Uncle. And you must kiss
Madame too. It's all over, it's all forgotten. . . . What I
mean is, everything's fine. You can imagine how
happy I am.

BARON: Alas, nephew! All is lost. The Grand Duchess of
Saxe-Coburg-Gotha is dead.

MARQUIS: Oh, too bad; and we just finished packing.

BARON: I just heard the terrible news a few minutes ago,
from Milord Duplessis.

COUNTESS: What, does this mean we're not going,
Valberg? And I had my heart set on it.

MARQUIS: Dear God! You won't leave me?

COUNTESS: No, but do take me somewhere.

MARQUIS: To Italy, madame, or Turkey, or Norway, or
anywhere you say.

BARON: Who could possibly have expected this appalling
catastrophe! All my arrangements were made, I had
His Majesty's letters, the gifts to present, it was all
prepared, all planned; and then the one thing you
never dreamed would happen . . .

MARQUIS: Well, you know the old proverb:
YOU CAN'T THINK OF EVERYTHING!